CONTENTS

THE CONTRIBUTORS

Jill Bourne is lecturer in Education at the Open University, where she has led the production of a new Primary Post Graduate Certificate in Education open learning course. She previously taught on the PGCE course at the University College of Swansea. She has written and lectured extensively on language in education, educational provision for bilingual pupils and the use of co-operative teaching strategies to bring about school improvement.

Lisa Dart is lecturer in Education at the University of Sussex. Her research interests are in teacher training and English education. Together with Pat Drake she has been researching patterns of mentoring in English and mathematics since 1991.

Pat Drake is currently Director of the Secondary PGCE course at the University of Sussex. Her interests are in mathematics education and gender, both internationally and at a national level. Together with Lisa Dart she has been researching patterns of mentoring in English and mathematics since 1991.

Vivienne Griffiths is a lecturer in Education at the University of Sussex, and Director of the Primary PGCE course. She also co-chairs the Primary Management Group on the recently established Sussex Consortium for Teacher Education and Research. She was formerly an advisory teacher for drama in West Yorkshire and has taught extensively in primary and secondary schools.

Jennifer Harrison has been a biology teacher in a Leicestershire upper school. She is currently a lecturer in Education at the University of Leicester School of Education, and Head of the Secondary PGCE course. At the time of writing she was a link tutor and science tutor in the PGCE secondary scheme. She is a member of the Partnership Steering Committee, with a responsibility and interest in the development of the school tutor training programme.

Chris Husbands is Reader in Education and Director of Post Graduate Teacher Education at the University of Warwick. He was previously senior lecturer in Education at the University of East Anglia, where the work on which the chapter in this collection was based was completed. He has research interests in the development of models of effective school-based teacher education and the links between initial teacher education and wider concerns of school and professional development.

Wayne Jones graduated in English from the University of Sussex before completing a PGCE at Brighton Polytechnic. He is currently co-ordinator of the Faculty of Communication at a comprehensive in East Sussex. He completed an MA in Curriculum Management and Development at the University of Sussex in 1993, mentoring forming the basis of his final dissertation. He has been closely involved with the University of Sussex PGCE scheme for four years.

Jenny Leach works as a staff tutor with the Open University's School of Education in the East Anglian region and co-ordinates the secondary English line of the OU's PGCE. She currently holds responsibility for the presentation of the OU PGCE in East Anglia, working closely with students, partner schools and mentors. Jenny has taught in schools in East Africa, Scotland and London and worked as an advisory English teacher in inner London.

Lynn D. Newton is a senior lecturer in Education (science) at the University of Newcastle and Director of the Primary PGCE course. She previously taught in primary schools in the North East, and was an advisory teacher for primary science and technology for Durham LEA.

Patricia Owen lectures in Education at the University of Sussex, and is history curriculum tutor on the Secondary PGCE course. She is also convenor of the part-time MA Women and Education. She was previously head of history and a PGCE mentor in a large comprehensive school in Crawley, West Sussex.

Kate Ring taught for five years in nursery and primary classes in the London Borough of Haringey. In 1990 she joined the full-time staff of the National Union of Teachers, and is currently acting Principal Officer for primary and middle schools in the Union's Education/Equal Opportunities department. Her remit includes working on the Union's policy in relation to Initial Teacher Education.

Susan Sanders is lecturer in mathematical education at the University of Wales, Swansea. She is also director of the PGCE (Primary) course. She was previously senior advisory teacher for mathematics for the City of Birmingham. She has also taught extensively in primary schools.

Paul Stephens is a practising teacher and head of sociology and social sciences in a large Leeds comprehensive school. He is also a writer on teaching and mentoring, a mentor to student teachers from the University of York, and a visiting lecturer there in Educational Studies.

Janice Windsor is an assistant deputy head at a large comprehensive school in West Sussex, where she is responsible for all matters to do with staff training and development as well as teaching English at GCSE and A-level. She leads three teams of enthusiastic mentors as well as training colleagues who wish to become mentors.

DEDICATIONS

In memory of my father Brian Rourke Griffiths and for my son Chris.

Vivienne Griffiths

For John and for Tom – with special thanks for all your efforts with my disk drive.

Patricia Owen

ACKNOWLEDGEMENTS

We should like to thank all the contributors to this volume, who worked so hard to ensure that it finally came to fruition; and especially Kate Ring who stepped in at half past the eleventh hour to ensure that it also contained a trade union contribution. Heartfelt thanks also to colleagues in the University of Sussex Institute of Education (USIE), in particular to Tony Becher, and to everyone in the Teacher Education office, especially Lorna and Shirley for all their help. We would also like to record our appreciation of the support and constructive advice received from colleagues in the Women's Cluster.

Thanks also to Anthea Millett for her helpful comments and provision of information for the writing of the final chapter. Thanks also to Marianne Lagrange for her encouragement and continued faith in our capacity finally to come up with the goods.

SECTION ONE
An Overview of Partnership

1

DEVELOPMENTS IN SCHOOL-BASED TEACHER EDUCATION

Vivienne Griffiths and Patricia Owen

INTRODUCTION

Recent government circulars on initial teacher education (DES, 1992; DFE, 1993a), which stress the need to develop partnerships between schools and training institutions, and a greater school involvement in the training of newly qualified teachers, are sometimes reported as though they are new developments in teacher education. However, they are by no means new ideas or practices. As long ago as 1944 the McNair Report proposed that teachers in schools 'should be primarily responsible for directing and supervising' students on teaching practice (McNair, 1944, para. 261) and advocated more practical work in schools during training courses. What becomes quite clear when looking back over the past twenty to thirty years is that partnerships and school-based training have been steadily evolving during this period, through professional initiatives and government legislation.

In this introductory chapter an overview of these developments will be given, including the most recent in this rapidly changing field. An initial analysis of some of the tensions and problems of implementation which a move towards more school-based initial teacher education (ITE) often brings about will also be included. Case studies of the ways in which different schools and institutions are developing new initiatives and tackling some of these problems will be described in detail in the remainder of the book. A summary of these will be given towards the end of this chapter.

CHANGES IN INITIAL TEACHER TRAINING 1965–1985

One of the main changes in ITT during this period was a move away from a division between theory and practice, towards a more integrated approach with more school involvement. In 1965 most teacher training students took three-year Teachers' Certificate courses at colleges of education, with a minority following the one-year Post Graduate Certificate in Education (PGCE), mainly based at universities. These courses largely followed the pattern of periods in college learning theory, which was then applied in school during teaching practices. Educational theory, and specialised subject studies, were paramount, with teaching methods courses having a lower status and classroom practice a long way behind (Bell, 1981). Although schools were used for the students' teaching practices, the teachers were not formally involved to any great extent in the students' development or assessment.

An exception at this time was the innovative school-based PGCE course at Sussex University which, from 1965 onwards, placed students for two-thirds of the year in schools, and involved teachers in schools as teacher tutors (what most courses now call mentors) with large responsibility for the guiding and assessing of students. The Sussex scheme emphasised the importance of the 'theorising teacher' (Wilkin, 1990, p. 7) and the development of the 'reflective practitioner' (Schon, 1983), rather than an apprenticeship model or 'sitting with Nellie' (Lacey and Lamont, 1975, p. 3). That is, the teacher tutor was seen as a vital and active partner in the professional development of teachers.

This kind of integrated approach was embodied in the James Report (DES, 1972), which proposed cycles of professional development with initial or pre-service training as the first stage. The James Report stressed the need for interdependence of schools and higher education institutions (HEIs) at all stages, and in particular proposed close links between colleges and schools in both the planning and delivery of ITE:

> The (colleges) would form a new and closer relationship with schools . . .
> The schools and the teachers in them would be asked to undertake new roles in teacher training . . . Teachers in schools would be more closely involved . . . in planning and supervising practical work . . . they should be associated with the selection of students.
> (DES, 1972, paras. 3.45 and 3.47)

Such proposals for closer collaboration between HEIs and schools, and a much enhanced role for teachers in schools, reflected moves in the colleges of education towards more school-based ITE, but represented radical changes in the university sector, where courses such as the Sussex PGCE remained the exception. The James Report criticised many university-validated ITE courses for being 'too academic' (ibid, para. 5.17), and saw the divide between theory and practice as iniquitous.

The next ten years saw a more widespread move towards partnership in practice, reflecting a growing dissatisfaction with educational theory, at first largely in colleges of education but later also in university departments of education (UDEs). The dominance of the subject disciplines came to be seen not only as irrelevant to classroom practice (Wilkin, 1990), but as inadequate in guiding and preparing students (Sutton, 1975; Wilson and Pring, 1975). Alongside these criticisms a professionalisation of teaching and teacher education was taking place, and teacher training courses started to reflect this in an increased emphasis on professional or teaching methods courses, and an upgrading in status of these elements, with the subject disciplines informing and supporting effective teaching, but not so important in their own right (Bell, 1981). The importance of classroom teachers' practical theories alongside the subject disciplines began to be recognised by educational philosophers such as Hirst (1979). Furlong *et al.* (1988) summarise this as a move from the 'application of theory' to a 'reflection in action' model (1988, p. 203).

Margaret Wilkin (1987) argues that this critical debate was not just taking place in the training institutions and among academics, but was also apparent among teachers themselves. Moves towards professionalism and more practical training approaches were strongly supported by the teacher unions (see Chapter 11), as well as by the validating body at that time, the Council for National Academic Awards (CNAA). With this fourfold support the role of school experience grew in importance, and many courses were redesigned in order to strengthen the partnership with schools and to give teachers a greater role.

During this time B.Ed. courses were being established, and PGCE courses were becoming the major route into teaching for secondary teachers. Most PGCE courses at UDEs were still traditional in approach and resistant to teachers in schools taking on more responsibilities (Patrick *et al.*, 1982). However, this was not the case at all UDEs. Apart from Sussex, where the school-based approach was still strongly affirmed, a rather different school-based model began to evolve at East Anglia based on teacher-researcher and action research approaches (Stenhouse, 1975; Elliott, 1976), as Chris Husbands will elaborate in Chapter 2. These and other school-based initiatives became the focus of government attention and DES-commissioned research (Furlong *et al.*, 1988).

The Conservative government supported moves towards school-based ITE, but for very different reasons from the schools and HEIs: government focus was on opening up education and teacher training to market forces. The White Paper *Teaching Quality* (DES, 1983) proposed closer links between training institutions and schools, and 'the active participation of experienced practising school teachers' (ibid:) in the training process. Circular 3/84 (DES, 1984) took these ideas further:

> Experienced teachers from schools, sharing responsibility with the training institutions for the planning, supervision and support of students' school experience and teaching practice should be given an influential role in the assessment of students' practical performance. They should also be involved in the training of students within the institutions.
>
> (DES, 1984, annex para. 3)

The Circular set out various requirements such as the length of time students were to spend in schools, which courses had to fulfil in order to be validated by the new Council for the Accreditation of Teacher Education (CATE), the body that replaced the CNAA. Unlike the James Report, which was leading the way in many of the ideas it put forward about ITE and in-service, Circular 3/84 was reflecting and thus legitimising ideas and practices which were already becoming well established. Rather than simply recommending possible changes, Circular 3/84 set out mandatory requirements and 'transferred into the political domain what previously had been a matter of professional debate and decision' (Wilkin, 1990, p. 4).

Furlong *et al.* (1988) suggest that one of the motives behind the 1984 legislation may have been a wish to undermine the role of HEIs in ITE. In most respects, however, the government view at this point largely coincided with that of the professionals. By the mid-1980s partnership arrangements were becoming very well developed in some HEIs, although they remained limited in others. Over the next ten years the picture was to change again, with government and professional views of partnership diverging, and the balance of power being shifted further towards the schools.

RECENT DEVELOPMENTS 1985–95

Over the last ten years changes in the educational and economic climate have been enormous, and have had inevitable repercussions on teacher training and on schools. The advent of the National Curriculum following the Education Reform Act of 1988, the introduction of national testing procedures, and local management of schools, have all had a profound effect on teachers' workload, particularly at primary level where staffing and resources are small. The continuing economic recession and government policy have meant no corresponding increase in resources to alleviate the strain of implementing these changes. It is hardly surprising that the accumulation of pressures on teachers led to the boycott of Key Stage 1 Standard Assessment Tasks (SATs) in 1993 and 1994, and calls for the slimming down of the National Curriculum which led to the Dearing Report (Dearing, 1993) and a revised National Curriculum to be introduced from September 1995.

It is within this context that major changes in ITE have been introduced and, perhaps unsurprisingly, tensions between government policy and professional views have become apparent. During this time HEIs have moved further away from a theory-practice divide towards an integrated approach. The Oxford Internship Scheme, developed between 1987 and 1990, exemplified this move. This scheme is based on the principle of complementarity: that each side of the partnership between school and university has a distinctive but equally important contribution to make in the training process. The scheme 'embodies a respect for and a questioning of both the craft knowledge and practical wisdom of practising teachers and also the more systematised and abstract knowledge of university tutors' (McIntyre, 1990, p. 31). The Oxford scheme is not only integrated in intent but in practice: the course is jointly planned by both university and school tutors (mentors), so that 'shared understandings' (McIntyre, 1988, p. 111) and 'agreement about intentions' (Eggleston, 1985, p. 183) underlie each aspect of the course. The Oxford model can be seen as the culmination of previous moves towards partnership, starting from the Sussex scheme in the 1960s, but articulated and extended within the context of the 1980s and 1990s.

Whilst at one level government policy has apparently been moving in a similar direction, towards closer partnership arrangements and more school-based training, the underlying principles of legislation on ITE over the last ten years have shown a marked difference from professional developments. Although superficially similar, government initiatives such as the Licensed Teacher (DES, 1988) and Articled Teacher (DES, 1989a) schemes have been clearly founded on an apprenticeship model, with an emphasis on the acquisition of skills or competences rather than the development of practice through critical reflection. Ted Wragg (1990) identifies a central tension between this apprenticeship approach and the continuing professional development (CPD) of teachers through initial training and further in-service, favoured by teachers themselves. In particular, the role of HEIs has been gradually undermined by recent legislation: in Circular 24/89 (DES, 1989b) schools emerge as the more powerful partner, with more direct responsibility for training (mentoring) rather than simply supervising students (Wilkin, 1992). These moves have culminated in the setting up of school-centred consortia for ITE (SCITT, DFE, 1993b), in which schools take the lead in planning and providing ITE, with or without the validation of HEIs.

Two recent circulars (DFE, 1992 and 1993a) have provided the main focus for government changes in the provision of ITE, and have had important repercussions for both schools and HEIs.

Circular 9/92

The planning and management of training courses should be the shared responsibility of higher education institutions and schools in partnership.
(DES, 1992, Annex A 1.2)

The DES circular on Initial Teacher Training (Secondary Phase), number 9/92 as it immediately became universally known, (35/92 in Wales), presents new procedures for both primary and secondary phase teacher training, and new criteria specifically for the secondary phase. One of the major principles highlighted in 9/92 as fundamental to the new arrangements is that schools should play a much larger part as full partners in initial teacher education. The requirement for school-based partnerships to become the norm in the provision of secondary teacher education is given clear precedence in the

circular. Moreover, the amounts of time which trainee teachers are required
to spend in their 'partner' schools (the DES's own designation) is clearly laid
down: eighteen, twenty-four, or thirty-two weeks depending on the type and
duration of the training course. Trainees are required to have the opportunity to
observe good primary as well as secondary teaching, as well as developing their
capacity for teaching their specialist subject alongside experienced teachers at
secondary level, and must 'have the opportunity to practise teaching in at least
two schools during their training' (ibid. Annex A).

The circular specifies that joint overall responsibility for all aspects of the
course is expected to be assumed by both sides of each ITE partnership,
including the provision of 'formal opportunities for (ITE) students to share their
self-assessment with tutors and mentors' (ibid., Annex B). However, within
this framework schools and HEIs are to accept different emphases. Course
accreditation procedure, certification and placement of trainees is to remain
the province of HEIs, whereas schools and colleges have the responsibility for
ensuring the development of subject and classroom based competence. HEIs are
required to show in their development plans for ITE courses a firm and clearly
delineated commitment to effective school-based partnerships. Following from
this there is thus an obligation for all participants in such partnerships to make
clear their joint plans for meeting the required criteria, including details of how
specific components of ITE courses are to be assigned between the partners,
and how appropriate funding for these components is to be allocated.

Circular 14/93

Schools should play a much larger and more influential role in course
design and delivery, in partnership as appropriate with higher education
institutions.

(DFE, 1993a, p. 5)

Like 9/92, DFE circular 14/93 (62/93 in Wales) sets out a 'greater role for
schools, which are best placed to help student teachers develop and apply
practical teaching skills' (ibid., p. 3). However, one significant difference is
that schools are no longer required to work in partnership with HEIs; they
may do so 'as appropriate' (ibid.) or take the lead by setting up their own
school-centred schemes (SCITT, DES, 1993b). The balance is clearly shifted
towards schools, as is the emphasis on 'practical teaching skills' alongside
subject knowledge. Nevertheless, the considerably increased time specified for
the teaching of the three core subjects, English, maths and science (150 hours
directed time on each instead of 100 hours), contains a strong implication,
although not directly spelt out, of heavy HEI involvement. Criteria are set
out, as in 9/92, for the meeting of new requirements, including the teaching
competences expected of newly qualified teachers.

Another important aspect of 14/93 is the proposal for 'high quality and cost
effective routes into primary teaching' (ibid., p. 4), and greater diversity of

course models, including a new three-year, six-subject B.Ed., and courses for teachers to become subject specialists at Key Stage 2. An original proposal to train unqualified mature students to teach at Key Stage 1, dubbed the 'Mum's Army' by the media, was vehemently opposed as undermining not only the status and professionalism of teachers, but also the skills needed to teach basic literacy and numeracy, and was dropped in the final version.

Among the alternative routes into teaching mentioned in the circular are the encouragement of mature students through the accreditation of prior learning and the setting up of certificated courses for classroom assistants.

ISSUES FOR PARTNERSHIP

In both circulars 9/92 and 14/93 the government has spelt out, to a greater degree than ever before, the requirements for teacher training courses and the criteria which have to be met before accreditation of any ITE course is granted. This marks the culmination of a steadily increased series of interventions, alongside the vastly increased state control of education through the introduction of the National Curriculum, national testing and school league tables. As John Furlong writes:

> Through their growing intervention in ITT, the government are claiming a right to control more than the hours teachers work; they are claiming the right to control more than what teachers teach . . . the government are claiming the right to have a say in the very construction of the professionality of the next generation of teachers, to determine what they learn, to determine how they learn it and to determine the professional values to which they are exposed.
>
> (Furlong, 1994, p. 11)

Understandably, such a degree of power and control brings about tensions and problems, as well as possible advantages. A number of issues of immediate concern arise, particularly around practical and structural aspects of partnership such as course content, school placements and resourcing. However, in dealing with these it is important not to lose sight of the longer-term professional issues around changes of role for teachers and HEI tutors, training needs and continuing professional development. Some of these areas will be discussed briefly below, as well as being taken up in more detail in later chapters.

Although, according to 9/92 and 14/93, all schools and colleges concerned with the education of pupils from the ages of 4 to 19 are expected to consider the possibility of involvement in ITE, the government puts the onus for the organisation and financing of partnerships firmly on to the schools and HEIs themselves. Schools and colleges wishing to offer initial teacher training places are expected to approach HEIs in the first instance, and HEIs are required to formulate and disseminate to schools their own individual criteria for the formation of partnerships, including indicators for evidence of quality of teaching and learning.

Schools in their turn are expected to provide information and evidence to HEIs of their suitability as initial teacher training institutions and of their proposed arrangements for the development of courses relevant to the needs of trainees. References to schools' expertise and 'track record' in providing staff development training for existing staff are of special significance in this respect, along with the wider school provision and facilities available, in particular the provision for special needs education and for extra-curricular activities. Having been offered these facilities by schools, the wording of both 9/92 and 14/93 make it clear that HEIs must be very sure of their ground if they subsequently turn down the school or college as a suitable training institution, and the penalty for doing so without very good reason is stringent:

> Where HEIs do not accept a school's offer of partnership, they should make clear the reasons for their decision. The Secretary of State reserves the right to withhold approval from an institution's courses of initial teacher training if there were evidence that individual schools had been treated arbitrarily or unreasonably.
>
> (DES, 1992, p. 4)

Reading such a statement the impression is formed of schools and colleges eager to offer their premises, and the time and services of their staff, to the implementation of school-based initial teacher training, only to be thwarted by HEIs' unwillingness to yield some of their perceived hegemony in ITE to the schools. Such an implication could well provoke a hollow laugh from schools and HEIs. In the three years which have elapsed since the issue of 9/92, rather than having to turn away large numbers of eager potential partnership schools, latest information collected by the Universities Council for the Education of Teachers (UCET, 1995) indicates that HEIs are experiencing very real problems in finding school or college placements for all their ITE students, particularly on secondary courses.

Such difficulties are freely acknowledged by schools as stemming from their reluctance and even inability to squeeze yet another function into a tightly overloaded schedule, or to ask willing and highly competent but already very busy teachers, who would undoubtedly make excellent mentors, to overburden themselves still further by taking on yet one more task for which inadequate time and funding is provided. The problem of finding school placements has also arisen on primary courses. Primary schools in particular are already hard pressed to meet all the heavy demands from the National Curriculum. With their smaller size, and consequently smaller resources, their good will may be stretched to the limit if they are expected to take on further responsibilities for ITE as well. Added to this, most primary teachers already hold co-ordinators' roles and see their primary purpose as educators of young children.

Reluctance to engage in the new arrangements for partnership-based models of initial teacher training thus comes in many cases not from HEIs unwilling to surrender their power, but rather more from schools where the importance of their involvement in school-based ITE is acknowledged, but where it is felt to be unreasonable and in fact impossible for a professional and acceptable job to be done, given the time and resources available. Thus in one important respect the proposed arrangements for partnership between schools and HEIs enshrined in 9/92 and 14/93 already appear somewhat distant from the reality in practice.

One interesting indication of this situation is the lack of take up by schools of the school-centred SCITT scheme (DES, 1993b); in September 1994 only twenty school-led consortia across the country in both primary and secondary ITE had been set up. The fact that none was sufficiently established to offer a chapter for this book also suggests that there is a long way to go before this particular scheme gets off the ground.

Funding lies at the heart of this problem. It is probably in the resourcing arrangements given in 9/92 and 14/93 that the greatest difficulties for successful development of partnership models of teacher training may be discerned. In both circulars the transfer of resources from HEIs to partnership schools is assumed, with arrangements to be negotiated locally, although under circular 14/93 schools taking the lead in ITE receive their funding directly from the government. Acknowledgement of probable future difficulties in this area is apparent, with the Secretary of State's stated intention to monitor developments closely, but apart from this promise, the question of further financial provision is left vague. Since 1994 the responsibility for funding ITE has been transferred to the newly established Teacher Training Agency, which is to conduct a survey of funding, but this will take time to complete.

Following the publication of 9/92 funding has, in fact, caused some of the most serious concerns about the implementation of partnership. Many HEIs used the transitional funding awarded to secondary courses from 1992–4 to transfer payments to secondary schools for their greater involvement in ITE, but this placed considerable strain on HEIs when the transitional funding came to an end. It also left highly diminished budgets available to fund the equivalent changes in primary ITE when these came into force. The funding arrangements (or lack of them) for primary courses are now leading to serious problems. Unlike the transitional funding provided for changes in secondary courses, transitional funds for primary ITE cannot be used by HEIs to transfer resources to schools. This means that there are no available funds without making cuts elsewhere in an already hard pressed HEI budget. The discrepancy between the funding of primary and secondary courses is now a national problem.

The implication of circular 14/93 is that HEIs should make cuts in their own provision in order to make adequate transfer of resources to schools. Transitional funding is earmarked 'to help schools prepare for their increased role, and to allow higher education institutions to readjust to take account of their changed responsibilities' (DFE, 1993a, p. 13). Whilst schools have a clearly 'increased role', HEIs will have to 'readjust' to 'changed responsibilities'; the implicit assumption here is that this will result in a lesser role for HEIs, although this contradicts the earlier requirement for increased core time on courses. Thus HEIs are caught in a dilemma about how to meet increased requirements from a dwindling pot. Schools are equally squeezed in all directions and are reluctantly having to make decisions about what to prioritise. In these circumstances ITE may be the area to be dropped by schools, and HEIs may have to pull out of ITE because they cannot meet the understandable demands for resources from schools, as the UCET survey indicates (1995).

This is a worst case scenario, arising out of new requirements as yet unsupported by additional funding. However, there are also many positive developments stemming from a move to school-based training and more clearly developed partnerships, particularly in the area of CPD. Some of these will be discussed in detail during the course of the book. Benefits include enhanced co-operation between HEIs and schools, and a greater understanding of each other's role in ITE. As the report of Her Majesty's Inspectorate of Schools *School-based Initial Teacher Training* (HMI, 1991) stresses, there are important issues of improving quality here:

> The concept of school-based training should not merely be a quantative one but should include also the quality of teacher involvement in planning, providing and assessing training and the quality of co-operation between higher education and schools.
>
> (HMI, 1991, para. 76)

Examples of such quality provision being developed through reciprocal support and complementarity between HEIs and schools are described in subsequent chapters. Such initiatives are often the result of years of previous course development along school-based lines (e.g. the courses at East Anglia, Leicester and Sussex, Chapters 2, 3 and 10), rather than a sudden response to government mandates, although other courses (e.g. Newcastle, Chapter 6) are taking the opportunity of new requirements to introduce major changes.

The other main area of substantial development through partnership is in mentoring, which, like partnership itself, has evolved over the last fifteen years or more as a vital part of the ITE process, as well as an important part of teachers' own professional development. In the HMI report (1991) the benefits of good mentoring to trainee teachers are clearly identified. The role of mentor is a complex one, requiring many personal and professional skills. There is certainly no shortage of books on aspects of mentoring (Wilkin, 1992; McIntyre *et al.*, 1993; Smith and West-Burnham, 1993; Yeomans and Sampson, 1994), reflecting the importance with which this is now regarded and the need for anaylsis of what makes an effective mentor. There is evidently a continuing need for more research on this area, particularly in primary education, and for accounts of mentoring from the schools' and the mentors' perspectives. Later chapters in this book (7, 8 and 9) provide examples of such school viewpoints.

OUTLINE OF SCHOOLS IN PARTNERSHIP

In Section Two, *Partnerships: Policy into Practice*, some different possible models of partnership between schools and HEIs at both primary and secondary levels are explored. This section stresses the structural, practical and intellectual aspects of partnership, and describes a number of different schemes which have been implemented in response to new training requirements, as well as continuing developments in existing school-based courses.

In the chapter by Chris Husbands an action research model for teacher education at the University of East Anglia, building on a long-established tradition in this field, is described. The emphasis throughout is on a reflective model firmly grounded in the school, and on the central position of classroom-based action research. Distinctions between theory and practice are thus virtually impossible to make and traditional ITE roles are reconceptualised within a model of all partners as learners.

Jennifer Harrison looks at the processes of partnership within a continuing professional development model of ITE in Chapter 3. The evolution of the partnership scheme at Leicester since the late 1980s is examined in detail, with a focus on the development of the Professional course, and on subject programme related work undertaken by students in both school and HEI contexts. Above all, the emphasis is on joint planning and evaluation and collaborative project work.

In Chapter 4 Susan Sanders addresses the very different issues for partnership faced by small primary schools in Wales. Welsh schools are not subject to exactly the same requirements as English ones, nor will they be accredited by the TTA in the future. Nevertheless, some of the problems faced by the schools in this chapter will apply equally to schools elsewhere in Britain. Susan Sanders also makes a strong case for the benefits of using small schools in ITT partnerships.

An open learning approach to primary ITE is described by Jill Bourne and Jenny Leach in Chapter 5. The transformation of teacher education in terms of 'social geography' is discussed in relation to the new Open University PGCE course. This increases access for mature students across the country, and gives rise to particular partnership needs which are described in an evaluation of the experiences of some of the first cohort to sample this distance learning approach in practice. The implications for continuing professional development are also explored.

In Section Three, *Mentor Development and Support*, the focus moves to mentoring, the benefits and problems associated with it, and examples of good practice evolving in different parts of the country. Lynn Newton's chapter provides a bridge between this and the book's second section in describing the development of 'diagnostic monitoring' of teacher competences at Newcastle, and the move towards an enhanced role in assessment for the supporting teachers (the term used rather than mentors). Stages in a student teacher's development are analysed in terms of a CPD model, and the close evaluation of the new scheme shows how a move to closer partnership and an increased role for schools is supported in practice.

Chapter 7 is the first of three chapters written from a school perspective. Himself a mentor, Wayne Jones conducted some research on mentoring in both primary and secondary schools, and in his chapter discusses the main issues arising from this, using both the trainee teachers' and mentors' viewpoints. A particularly interesting aspect of Jones's findings is the analysis of the mentor-trainee relationship in terms of age and gender, and the implications this has for the success or otherwise of the experience on either side. The need for adequate time, funding and training to support effective mentoring is stressed, and the benefits of mentoring to the individual and the school are identified.

Paul Stephens also writes as a mentor and a school-based tutor. In Chapter 8 he emphasises the importance of ITE students' socialisation, not just into their teaching practice school but into the wider demands of a principled and committed professional approach. This goes beyond the mere training of students to achieve a set of teaching competences, and requires the development of sensitivity and receptivity of ITE students in schools to issues of conscience in their everyday classroom practice. As Stephens puts it: 'teachers are reflective too'.

In Chapter 9 Janice Windsor writes from the perspective of a school Professional Tutor, responsible for implementing mentor development and support. She describes the workings of mentor training and the way in which an ITE scheme is given prominence as an important part of staff development in a comprehensive school, enhancing the experience of all who come into contact with it.

Finally in this section Lisa Dart and Pat Drake analyse the intellectual demands which underpin effective mentoring, by focusing on subject mentoring on the Sussex secondary PGCE course. They argue that different philosophies and forms of professional knowledge held by experienced subject teachers will lead to differing interpretations of the criteria for subject knowledge and application in relation to trainee teachers. These issues are explored through a close analysis of interviews between mentors and trainees in English and maths, and the implications for a competency-based approach are highlighted.

In the final section, *Looking Ahead*, Kate Ring of the National Union of Teachers (NUT) traces the evolution of school-based ITE in the context of the largest teaching union's approach and response to these developments. The safeguarding of the interests of all participants in school-based ITE, and the important contribution which properly organised and funded schemes can make towards improving the experience of everyone involved in whatever aspect of education, are also central themes in the NUT contribution.

In conclusion the editors draw together, in Chapter 12, some of the main issues arising from previous chapters in order to summarise the strengths and weaknesses of school-based ITE and to indicate ways forward for partnerships. The remit and aims of the recently established Teacher Training Agency (DFE, 1994), and the implications this has for future funding, accreditation and research in teacher education, are also analysed.

The context for current developments in partnership is one of rapid change; schools have already become well adapted to this in recent years, and HEIs are having to make similar adjustments. It is particularly important to keep a sense of perspective, seeing current changes as one more step in a long history of developments in ITE, rather than as a sudden intervention on the part of the government. It is also vital to maintain a sense of professional autonomy and control, and for HEIs and schools to see this as an opportunity to improve the quality of teacher education through a deeper understanding of each others' strengths and the forging of closer relationships.

This book does not attempt to provide a definitive blueprint for successful partnership, because so many aspects are context-dependent and different factors will emerge as important from place to place, forming a unique configuration. However, it will hopefully provide some information and food for thought, as well as useful guidelines and examples of good practice, for those engaged in the vital business of educating the next generation of teachers on both sides of the partnership.

NOTE

We have used the term initial teacher education (ITE) in preference to initial teacher training (ITT) as the former is now more commonly used. However, we refer to initial training where it makes more sense to do so, and some of the other contributors to this volume have used ITT.

SECTION TWO

Partnerships: Policy into Practice

2

LEARNING TEACHING IN SCHOOLS: STUDENTS, TEACHERS AND HIGHER EDUCATION IN A SCHOOL-BASED TEACHER EDUCATION PROGRAMME

Chris Husbands

INTRODUCTION

Research and Knowledge on Teacher Education

What are the implications of 'partnership' models of teacher education for the three key stakeholders in initial teacher education: students, higher education institutions and schools themselves? The effective management of teacher education has typically been problematic, involving the successful 'meshing' of different concerns of students, their higher education institutions and their placement schools. McIntyre (1987) highlights a series of problems which have traditionally afflicted conventional models of initial teacher education. Taken together they can be characterised as relating in different ways to the student teachers themselves, to schools and to supervising tutors in institutions of higher education. For students there are fundamental problems in learning to teach in higher education institutions and, in parallel, in placement schools: relating what is learnt in higher education to the classroom is challenging. Few students, notes McIntyre, make explicit use of the ideas, theories and concepts to which they have been introduced in higher education. Some element of this difficulty arises from students' inability to reconcile conflicting advice and ideas from supervising tutors and from teachers in placement schools (Elliott, 1991); moreover, students are generally reluctant to regard classroom practice and curriculum as problematic (Tickle, 1987). Other difficulties arise from student teachers' difficulties in reconciling their own preconceptions about teaching and learning, new approaches which they may be introduced to only fleetingly in practice schools or their higher education institution, and the pressure to develop coping strategies in the classroom (Lacey, 1977).

In schools teacher education has generally received little systematic attention, but there are problems for students in relating the specifics of their curricular, pastoral and institutional practice to theoretical conceptions of curriculum, classroom practice and pastoral care to which they will have been introduced in more general lectures and seminars in higher education. Furlong *et al.* have identified a series of levels (Furlong *et al.*, 1988) or dimensions (Furlong and Maynard, 1993) which characterise students' learning in relation to teaching. Of these dimensions the first, 'practical classroom practice', can only be experienced in placement schools, but different practices and policies in different schools can produce difficulties for students in integrating the different 'dimensions' of professional learning. McIntyre (1987, p. 105) notes, in addition, 'that students generally do not learn much, although there is a great deal to be learned, from their observation of experienced teachers'. For higher education tutors constraints of time and logistics mean that they cannot visit student teachers sufficiently often for their visits to relate closely to student teachers' own agendas for continuous development through target setting. In addition their inability to relate immediately to complex and variable contexts within which student teachers' practice takes place creates problems for the relation of their supervisory comments to the student teacher's perception of that context, although, of course, the ability to offer de-contextualised comment may have other benefits.

At both ideological and professional levels the thrust of government reforms in teacher education since 1984 has been to attempt to resolve these difficulties by enhancing the role of the school in initial teacher education (Wilkin, 1993). However, as McIntyre (1987) suggests, both the diagnoses of the endemic problems of teacher education and the nature of curriculum development in schools and higher education over the last fifteen years are likely to produce a range of different curricular and administrative structures in initial teacher education. Teacher education might be grounded on an apprenticeship-based model, in which fundamental responsibility for student learning was transferred to 'master teachers' who took oversight of students' acquisition of practical teaching skills: this is a model which has considerable political and ideological currency, particularly among commentators on the right (Lawlor, 1990; Clarke, 1992), though not exclusively so (Hargeaves, 1990). Equally, the diagnosis might support an IT-INSET approach to initial teacher education in which higher education tutors led both student teachers and their placement teachers in the exploration of new pedagogical and curricular ideas. In the 1980s such an approach received considerable support from teacher education institutions, most notably in Leicester and Exeter (Ashton, Henderson and Peacock, 1989). Or the diagnosis might support an internship model, as developed by McIntyre and others in Oxfordshire (McIntyre, 1987; Pendry, 1990). What is at issue in all such curriculum models are different conceptions of student teacher learning, and different conceptions of the respective roles of schools and higher education.

THE DEVELOPMENT OF AN ACTION-RESEARCH MODEL OF TEACHER EDUCATION AT THE UNIVERSITY OF EAST ANGLIA

This chapter describes a model of teacher education, built on the diagnoses of structural difficulties outlined above, and drawing on the details of a programme of teacher education and assessment developed at the University of East Anglia (UEA) between 1991 and 1993. Discussions on developing initial teacher education in the region, as a response to some of the structural difficulties of 'traditional' PGCE courses, had begun with small groups of headteachers and teachers in the mid-1980s (Brown, 1985; Halliwell, 1988), and again in 1991, but were given added urgency in the autumn of 1991 and spring of 1992, a time of rapid change in teacher education, as national policy accelerated the development of school-based, competency-led models of initial teacher education (Clarke, 1992; DFE, 1992). Certain features and traditions of the University and its region played an important part in the development of models of initial teacher education against the current research and national policy backgrounds. Most secondary schools in the region, outside the two major urban areas of Norwich and Ipswich, are relatively small (500–750 pupils) and headteachers were concerned that the model of initial teacher education adopted should not 'overload' their schools. In such schools 'faculty' rather than departmental structures are common and many teachers teach across a number of cognate disciplines. Headteachers further argued that the development of school-based initial teacher education should not, by default, exclude any schools or types of schools from participation in the professional preparation of student teachers, but that both rural and urban schools, both large and small schools, had a distinctive part to play in initial teacher education. These factors inhibited the adoption of an internship model (Benton, 1990).

In the University the tradition of action-research, and in particular the conceptualisation of professional development as grounded in systematic workplace inquiry, deriving from Stenhouse's advocacy of the 'teacher-as-researcher' (Stenhouse, 1975), has for some time played a central role in the thinking of the School of Education at the University of East Anglia and in award-bearing in-service provision (Elliott, 1985; Elliott, 1990). A considerable number of teachers in secondary schools in the region have undertaken in-service work at the University, and the concept of action-research is well developed in the region. Such a tradition disposed schools against apprenticeship models of initial training and against reductive interpretations of competency-based frameworks.

The strength of action-research traditions in the University and its neighbour schools provided a promising starting point for the development of school-based training for both schools and the University. Indeed, early work with headteachers suggested that they were strongly disposed towards developing school-based initial teacher education as far as possible within an action-research framework, grounded in the structured observation and investigation of classroom practice, in which the school is both the setting for classroom practice and the location of professional investigation. The programme of initial teacher education developed between the University and its regional schools reflects this shared concern.

Underpinning the programme are two linked concepts. The first is a conception of teaching as a research-based, reflective activity, in which observation, practice and research are closely linked. Students begin attachment to a placement school within a few days of registering on the PGCE programme, and early school-located experience is heavily weighted towards structured observation. Observation of practice, linked to a programme of development, analysis and reflection in higher education, continues throughout the course, but students' own practice plays an increasingly important role. Just as observation is structured, so is practice: team-teaching, small-group teaching, support teaching and whole-class teaching all play important parts. Students' learning from practice is supported in four ways:

- through their observation of, and work with, experienced teachers in school;
- through their observation of, and work with their subject partner in the school;
- through their analysis of and reflection on their own practice in support-teaching, small-group and whole-class work;
- and through the investigation and production, after their first period of 'block' placement, of a school-based research project.

Coherence and continuity are established through three components:

- the record of student experience, which constitutes the main information system in the programme;
- course development teams of higher education tutors and schoolteachers which have designed the structure of the programme;
- written detailed guidance on curriculum structure and assessment.

Unlike the Oxford 'internship' programme (Benson, 1990; McIntyre 1987, pp. 98–9) student learning is not centred on one school, but on two after an initial period of school observation: one in the first half of the year and one in the second, although the distribution of 'block' and 'serial' placement between the two schools varies. There are strictly practical reasons for this maximal interpretation of the guidance accompanying the DFE criteria for secondary training (CATE, 1992), which relates to the headteachers' concerns that their relatively small schools and small departments should not be overloaded with students.

The second fundamental concept underpinning the programme is that both schools and the University are equally concerned with practice and theory, indeed that a view of teaching as a research-based, reflective activity makes any effective distinction between the two impossible. Thus schools are the location for practice, but they are also places where practice is interrogated by students and by teachers working together: the guidance on observation and review of students' teaching produced by the University and a group of deputy headteachers takes the form of a series of 'prompt' questions. During the students' first placements, as a part of their submission for formal assessment, they compile an analytical dossier of observations and reflections on their own practice, their partners' practice and the practice of experienced teachers. Schools, however, are also places which interrogate and develop their own practice, and the second-term school-based research project is on a theme arising from students' placement school development plans, agreed in negotiation between students and the school and supervised not from the University but from the school. The University is equally concerned with both practice and the investigation of practice: the agreed course is organised through a series of questions about classroom practice, whole school policy and schooling. The core of the programme is practice as observed and experienced by the students in their placement schools, and the central task of the University programmes is to help student teachers to develop their understanding of, and facility in, classroom practice through accessing experienced teachers' craft knowledge (Brown and McIntyre, 1986) and, increasingly, an understanding of curriculum through processes of school development planning (Hargreaves and Hopkins, 1991). In this sense 'theory' is an inappropriate term to describe the concerns of higher education: the concern of the higher education component of the programme is with the investigation, analysis and refinement of classroom practice through case study and observation.

IMPLICATIONS FOR STUDENTS, SCHOOLS AND HIGHER EDUCATION

At root this structure accepts that 'there is not, nor can there be, any systematic corpus of theoretical knowledge from which prescriptive principles for teaching can be generated' (McIntyre, 1980, p. 296). Instead, 'learning to teach must be a continual process of hypothesis testing' (Alexander, 1984). It is entirely possible to develop a teacher education curriculum from such starting points within the outline (DFE, 1992) of a competency-based accreditation and assessment framework. The UEA programme grounds this hypothesis-testing in the observation and analysis of placement departments and in the systematic observation of a student's placement partner. From the beginning of the programme classroom-based hypothesis-generation and development lie at the core of student learning since 'the classroom is not only a place of work but also a source of professional development' (Thiessen, 1992, p. 86). Teacher learning is not straightforward (Calderhead, 1987), and 'teachers do not develop ... by themselves ... They learn most, perhaps from other teachers, particularly from colleagues in the workplaces, their own school. (But) there is no simple way for teachers to learn from their colleagues' (Hargreaves, 1992, p. 216). Students each have another student with whom to share responsibilities, observations and problems, and schools, students and the University exploit the potential of paired placements to the full in order to generate team teaching, observation of experienced classroom teachers and of each other. Early in the programme students undertake no teaching activities, and subsequently induction to teaching is structured and progressive. Guidance to students and schools makes it plain that observation and interrogation of the practice of experienced teacher is as valid at the end of the programme as it is at the beginning: whilst the agenda of observation may have altered, and the balance between practice and observation may have shifted, the principles of observation remain valid.

A central feature of the programme is the school-based research project which students undertake in pairs after they have completed a period of both serial attachment and block placement in a school. The timing and structure of the project are both important. In so far as it is possible within the constraints of the one-year initial teacher education programme, the students are by this time insider-researchers, with an implicit understanding of the institution in which they have been placed (Elliott, 1990). At the same time the research programme grows out of the school's own agenda for development because it arises from an issue of concern to the school: initial work with schools and with students suggests that both of these features of the project are extremely attractive. Schools regard the project as a valuable planning resource. Early planning for the programme went further in suggesting that the written products of the students' research project, in addition to being available to the school for further development planning, should have been assessed formally as student's coursework by a member of staff in the school, as a further way of breaking down the divisions between higher education staff and school staff and indicating clearly to students that both were equally concerned with reflection and writing. However, pressures in schools at a time of considerable change and difficulty for school management teams have postponed this element of the project.

The role of the school in initial teacher education has, in some ways, been hardest to specify. Conventional models of initial teacher education conceptualise the school as at a minimum providing a location for practice (Furlong *et al.*, 1988; Field, 1993), and recent developments have tended to move forward by enhancing the responsibility of schools (CATE, 1992) and by consolidating their involvement in the planning and development of programmes (McIntyre, 1987, pp. 112–13). The UEA model accepts both of these developments, and the programme builds on development work carried out by working groups throughout 1992 and 1993, as well as drawing on and consolidating earlier work (Brown, 1986). Beyond this the school here is seen as central to the process of initial teacher education. McIntyre (1994, p. 81) has suggested that 'classrooms are the dominant contexts for student teachers' learning', and whilst we would agree with the proposition, we would argue more generally that the school is the dominant context for learning. The school is not simply a place where students practise, but neither is it a place where they simply 'acquire' the skills of classroom teaching. The school is a place where classroom practice is interrogated, on the basis of systematic observation, enquiry and reflection. There are a number of reasons for conceptualising the role of the school in teacher education at school rather than classroom level, some of which derive from the principles underpinning the programme and others from the development in the United Kingdom and elsewhere of conceptions of school-based review and evaluation (Clift and Nuttall, 1987; Caldwell and Spinks, 1989). The notion that teacher development is conducted on the basis of inquiring into teachers' own practice (Elliott, 1990) lies at the centre of the programme developed by schools and the University. More than this the explicit concern with inquiry into the practice of schooling recognises the reality of 'thinking schools' and makes plain to students through their involvement in school-based research that school development is central to the practices of schooling in the 1990s.

An important feature of recent work on teaching has been the development and extension of the concept of the 'mentor', whose task has generally been conceptualised as taking responsibility for the detailed planning of student programmes and accessing for students teachers' own professional craft knowledge, and with whom students might enjoy a secure personal relationship (McIntyre, 1987, p. 107; Wilkin, 1993; Hagger and McIntyre, 1993). This development has in turn engendered an extensive literature on mentoring qualities, skills and responsibilities, and an acceptance of the role and adoption of the nomenclature of mentoring is apparent in national policy guidelines (DFE, 1992; CATE 1992). However, there are a number of ways in which the action-research based programme described has shifted emphasis from the central role of a mentor. This is not because the programme does not accept that fundamental to learning to teach is a structure which allows students to access the professional craft knowledge of experienced teachers. McIntyre defines the role of the mentor as 'co-ordinat(ing) the classroom related learning experiences of each intern (= student) throughout the year' (1987, p. 98), and the adoption of a two-school teacher education model makes such security of relationship between students and mentors impossible. Teachers in schools, however, do have access to the context-bounded knowledge of classroom learning in their own school on which any development of individual practice depends. Some headteachers indicated to us that they felt that they wished to widen the concept of the role of mentor, and to think rather in terms of the school as a mentoring institution, in which students related to a range of other experienced teachers in ways which reflected the needs of the student and the strengths of the school: at some times the critical relationship would be between the student and a teacher in the student's own teaching subject, at other times it might be with a learning support co-ordinator or an information technology co-ordinator. In smaller schools especially, headteachers wished to capitalise on particular strengths of experienced teachers, operating across the range of disciplines.

For these reasons the 'mentor' plays a less central role in the UEA programme than in some other developing models of teacher education, and schools retain the flexibility to manage school-located components of initial training as they wish providing that a clear structure is in place for the coherent management of student learning. More attention has instead been focused on the sorts of learning and professional experiences which schools need to provide in order to support the development of new teachers' classroom competences. We have found it helpful to classify these experiences under four generic headings both for schools and for students.

1. Students need access to variations of basic procedures, frequently at the most 'basic' of levels: opportunities to collect variations on ways of beginning or ending a lesson, opportunities to collect variations of approaches to assessing and evaluating pupils' work, and so on.
2. Students need opportunities to experiment with styles and structures, opportunities to develop novel ways of working with them. This is as likely to be developed through the opportunity to explore learning in different curriculum areas as through the exploration of mentor practices in a student's own teaching specialism.
3. Student teachers need encouragement to make and test hypotheses about classrooms and learning in order to develop their own practices.
4. Finally, of course, students need opportunities for direct practice. At this level the programme has an explicit concern with mentoring generically conceived, rather than with the role of a 'mentor', with the possible implications, identified by McIntyre, that a preoccupation with the role of mentors might produce an over-emphasis on 'modelling' behaviours (McIntyre, 1994)

In order to support schools' diversity of management the central components of student experience in the programme are the record of student experience, and the notes of guidance on school-university relationships produced by working groups of teachers and University staff. The responsibility for the management of both rests with a named senior member of school staff, but schools are developing their mentoring responsibilities in a number of ways.

The implications for the programme of teacher education developed here for tutors working in higher education are considerable; indeed, one obvious lacuna in recent work on school-based teacher education has been the absence of serious discussion on the changing role of higher education tutors. There is, for example, the potential for a series of 'boundary' disputes as tutors are required to recognise those components of student practice which are now the responsibility of schools rather than of higher education. In the same way there is the potential for schools to look to higher education for an articulation of the theoretical components of training and hence to widen the gap between a practical school-based initial training curriculum and a theoretical higher education curriculum. There are few easy or obvious solutions to the difficulties, and most of them need to be addressed through the development of the realities of 'partnership' as much as through the rhetoric of curriculum development. However, it may be that the scope for overt conflict can be reduced through the careful articulation of higher education's contribution to the development of new teachers' competence and professional learning. Within the programme described here, the University-based component of the programme is developed through two elements:

• a professional development strand, incorporating a focus on classroom methodology, whole-school policy concerns as they affect classroom practice and any issues not directly related to students' own subject teaching, including a core information technology programme;
• and a curriculum strand, incorporating work on students' main teaching subjects and, in the second term, a subsidiary teaching subject. In practice the teams of professional development tutors and curriculum tutors overlap considerably: all professional development tutors are also curriculum tutors.

The concern of these teams of tutors is with supporting the work of schools and students. Tutors support students' own development as classroom practitioners by drawing on and prompting students' investigation-based practice, by developing with schools and students ideas for classroom practice which will consolidate and extend students' practice, and by developing with students an understanding of curriculum, classroom processes and schooling which is situated in, and derives from, their experience in schools throughout the programme. Support for schools is co-ordinated by professional development tutors, each of whom has overall responsibility for liaison with a cluster of up to four schools, for the nature and coherence of students' programmes in those schools. Like teachers, both professional development and curriculum tutors are concerned with the establishment, development and extension of good practice and, like teachers, tutors will be concerned with the establishment of models of good practice to which individual students can relate and develop. However, the nature of the engagement with practice will be different for tutors as compared with classroom teachers, since tutors will have less knowledge of context and since they have readier access, both through their research obligations and the opportunity to bring students from a number of schools together, to opportunities for the articulation of the principles on which practice is based.

The programme of teacher education described here begins from a particular conception of teaching as a context-bounded, research-focused activity in which the development of classroom competence cannot be defined narrowly nor divorced from wider ideas about reflection and practice. As a result the framework negotiated between, and developed by, the University and schools re-conceptualises the roles of all three partners in teacher education. For students the programme accepts, as others have done, the need to recognise students' own agendas and conceptions of teaching (McIntyre, 1987; Alexander, 1980) as the basis for their development as accomplished classroom practitioners. For schools the programme accepts their central role in teacher education as the location of practice, and as the context in which discourse about practice and investigations into practice occur. For tutors in higher education the reconceptualisation is perhaps the most significant; if tutors in the past have regarded student teachers as 'their' students this model of teacher education re-defines the relationship quite considerably. Here, higher education-based tutors support and develop the work of school and students, and assist both in the investigation and articulation of good practice.

3

A RATIONALE FOR PARTNERSHIP: THE EVOLUTION OF A COURSE OF INITIAL TEACHER EDUCATION

Jennifer Harrison

UNDERSTANDINGS OF PARTNERSHIP

Education at every level is undergoing change all over the Western world. This is partly because we find shifting values and changing economic circumstances, and partly because we have increased knowledge about how we teach and learn most effectively. Such factors have brought about redefinitions of the goals and processes of teaching and learning. The implications for ITE are further complicated because, as teachers in schools today, we find we need a wide range of skills to meet the increasing demands made upon us. Teachers not only need to be committed and well-educated subject specialists and to be able to diagnose pupils' learning difficulties, but must also be able to help pupils with personal difficulties, and to communicate effectively with parents and governors. Some teachers ultimately take on responsibilities of leadership in a particular curriculum area or take a share of the responsibility for the financial management of the school. There is no doubt that there is a clear need for effective training and learning throughout professional teaching life, and that an important part of this is in the first year in initial teacher education.

Partnership should be viewed more widely than the obvious link between schools and a university department of education. Partnership can be defined as *linked activity*, with the most important factor in the equation being the student teachers, who bring with them a myriad of experiences and skills, many very relevant to teaching. There may be many different starting points among individuals and such a diverse group bring skills which can be built upon. Another partner in the equation is the body of pupils in school. All our common efforts are in the end directed towards giving pupils a richer and more rewarding experience during their time in school. Currently in ITE we are being asked to improve the quality of teaching in school, alongside the work we do with the student teachers (DFE, Circular 9/92), and certainly we need to encourage student teachers to concern themselves primarily with children's learning.

Learning of course takes place in situations other than schools, and is brought about by people other than teachers, and in places other than schools and colleges. Facilities such as zoos, museums, libraries, art galleries, theatres and concert halls promote life-long learning, and should be acknowledged despite their connections with pure recreation or high-brow intellectualism. In ITE we need to be able to help student teachers recognise the value of the experiences for their pupils which go beyond the classroom or laboratory: those which encompass the residential week, or the weeks of work experience, or an industrial placement. The place of work, churches, sports and recreation clubs, meeting rooms of unions and political parties all have a place in life-long learning. Student teachers could be part of the briefing and debriefing process of work experience with pupils; they could find out what pupils get out of the placements, what teachers get out of such placements, and likewise what industry or business get out of them! The crucial thing about these settings is to create specific goals so that the learning becomes self-directed and has a particular significance.

We need also to enable student teachers to realise that schools exist in communities and to place the school in which they work in such a context. Some student teachers experience for themselves residential work in the form of field activities, notably on science or geography courses. Indeed there is clearly a place for all student teachers to have such experiences, and to include in this the planning, negotiation and the management of such events. Devising links with the community is part of the partnership, and linked activities can provide a greater understanding of other people's skills, styles of management, better communication and a mutual regard for each other's efforts. Partnership, however, is more than a linked activity – it is clearly a *joint commitment*, of time, effort and resources to a venture designed to produce joint benefits.

When I consider the needs of student teachers during secondary ITE I think immediately of developing their confidence as subject specialists, and of developing their confidence as all-round professionals in the classroom and the school. To be wholly successful, therefore, ITE has to provide a number of opportunities which can allow the student teacher to:

• acquire basic teaching skills
• play a full part in the normal life of the school
• gain experience of working collaboratively with teachers to improve the quality of pupils' learning.

All of these have to be placed in the wider contexts of the life-long professional development of teachers and the processes of school improvement. We need to equip student teachers with the power of self-evaluation, and the professional skills with which to carry this out. There is therefore an important place for active classroom evaluation and a need for the development of the skills of a 'reflective practitioner'.

A HISTORY OF WORKING WITH SCHOOLS

A long tradition of school-based work in Leicestershire has preceded the more formal mechanisms now being put into place. Brian Simon was able to describe as early as 1966:

> a fruitful relationship between the university and practising teachers from different schools. For those acting as teacher-tutors in a particular subject – say history, biology or physics – may meet regularly for discussions at the School of Education, discussions which have extended to cover new developments in teaching the subject, research under way, as well as the tutorial function itself.
>
> (Simon, 1980, p. 86)

Later, in the 1980s, work was undertaken by Pat Ashton and colleagues under the title of IT-INSET (Initial Training-Inservice Training) in the Centre for Evaluation and Development in Teacher Education based at the University of Leicester. These identifiable influences have affected the development of the present Partnership scheme, which has been in existence since its launch as a pilot scheme in 1989.

The IT-INSET model exploited the motives of the various participants in which the driving force was the team of professionals. Such a team was composed of a teacher from the particular school in which the task was carried out, a group of PGCE student teachers, usually about six, and a university tutor. The class teacher had responsibility for the choice of the classroom focus, but thereafter the tasks carried out by the team members were shared:

> All members of the team participate in all aspects of the team's work:
>
> • they plan the work as a team;
> • they share the teaching and observations in the classroom;
> • they evaluate the relevance and value of what pupils have gained from each session;
> • they reflect on what has been learned;
> • they use this in the next planning stage.
>
> (Everton and Impey, 1989, p. 6)

The notion of the team approach was held to be a response to the guidance offered by CATE in helping the institutions meet the requirements of DES Circular 3/84.

The most effective partnership arrangements between institutions and schools are often those which have been designed with the needs of students, trainers and teachers equally in mind. The IT-INSET model, which is actually cited in Catenote No. 4 (CATE, 1986) does indeed address the needs of students, trainers and teachers equally.

(Everton and Impey, 1989, p. 3)

Pilot Partnership Model 1989–1991

The Partnership model was built upon these earlier relationships with local schools and evolved over a two-year pilot phase. The earlier experiences of co-operation and understanding between partners were crucial to the eventual apparent success of the Partnership scheme. Briefly the structure of the course and the arrangements for involving Partnership schools in the overall programme in 1989–91 were as follows: student teachers spent two days a week, when not on block teaching practice, in a particular cluster of partnership schools early in the autumn term, followed by a block practice in one of the schools in the cluster. A further two days a week were spent in the school in the spring term (followed by a second block practice in a different school), with a return to the Partnership cluster for three days per week in the second part of the summer term. The total time spent on school-based work was 60 per cent.

In the pilot phase about one-third of the PGCE secondary intake at Leicester – composed of student teachers in five subject areas – was involved with school-based work in a manner which ran alongside the traditional PGCE course. The Partnership arrangements covered two terms of the year, and created an opportunity for subject pairs of student teachers to spend a day a week (normally spent at the University) in the Partnership school. In addition student teachers were placed in these clusters of schools as a cross-curricular group, with a university tutor and the school's Professional tutor deciding, and playing a part in, a programme of professional issues. The clustering arrangement of schools was significant, both in the county and city schools (where there are age breaks for secondary pupils at 14 years and 16 years respectively) in providing student teachers with some direct, or indirect, contact with the whole secondary age range.

By 1992 fifty schools in Leicestershire and Northamptonshire were involved. They were grouped in 17 clusters to provide experiences of the 11–18 age range. Typically in the city a cluster consisted of two 11–16 schools and a sixth form college; in the county a cluster was two 11–14 high schools and a 14–18 upper school. About sixteen students were attached to each cluster, with between four and ten students per school from various subject specialisms.

In the second year of the pilot phase (1990–91), the extent of the Partnership arrangements doubled in terms of student teachers, schools and university tutors, reflecting in part the extent of the influence of the pre-existing relationships, and in part the willingness of the local Partnership schools to cope with arrangements which were sound but based, nevertheless, almost entirely on goodwill. In the summer term of 1991 external examiners found that student teachers in the Partnership schools were generally more enthusiastic about their experiences than the parallel set receiving more traditional training.

By 1991–92 the whole secondary PGCE course had moved over to the Partnership arrangements described above. Thus there was nearly three years' experience of the Partnership mode of working by the time the DES Circular 9/92 was to appear. Until this time it had been supported by Leicestershire LEA, using a limited level of funding available for teacher retention and recruitment. This was done in the knowledge that the majority of the new teacher recruits in the area were drawn from those local institutions running the PGCE.

Underlying Principles of Partnership 1991–92

1 Subject Specialism Links and the Wider Dimensions of the Teaching Role.

The course provided a holistic approach to professional development in that it made links between subject specialisms and the wider dimensions of the teaching role.

Wherever possible students worked as a pair attached to a subject department and collaborating closely with a designated teacher (the co-tutor), forming a team of three. This team planned, taught and discussed much of the work throughout the year. More particularly, student teachers worked early on with small groups of pupils, and both observed class teachers and were themselves observed, in a supportive atmosphere. The university subject tutor endeavoured to work closely with these school co-tutors to form a closely related subject programme at the university. Such a multitude of experiences in the various Partnership schools allowed for examination of the problems and insights during this university subject time.

As the year progressed the work of the subject team became more focused and more closely concerned with classroom evaluation. Examples of this type of collaborative project work generally reflected the current concerns of the science department, and science co-tutors became involved not only in the setting up and participation in this project, but also in the tutorial guidance and monitoring of it.

The second strand to the PGCE programme was the Professional Course, which was structured as a core of ten topics studied by all student teachers and concerned with whole-school issues of relevance to all student teachers regardless of subject specialism. It was intended that these two strands (subject work and Professional Course) should be experienced as part of an integral course. Whenever whole-school issues arose links could be established between the two. Wider dimensions such as equal opportunities, special educational needs, and personal and social education could be incorporated into subject work. This process was aided by the fact that the majority of university tutors had dual roles as subject tutors and Professional Course link tutors. Student teachers spent an equivalent of one day per week in school on subject work and one day on whole-school issues.

As with subject work the current concerns of the school did to some extent determine the Professional Course topics which were studied in depth. All student teachers were of course required to study these ten topics; in school some were chosen for study in more depth because of student preferences or as part of project work determined by the school to inform development planning in the school. There was considerable informal support here by the school's Professional tutor in negotiating work by the student teachers in different aspects of school life.

The teaching strategies adopted in the Professional Course were centred on a loose-leafed collection of materials on the ten Professional topics. They required independence in study and promoted links between university and school-based work. The student teachers had a weekly school-based seminar with the university Link tutor in which Professional Course topics could be discussed within the school context. The teaching and learning styles in school included the following strategies:

- independent self-directed study, singly or in small groups
- group presentations
- progress tutorials with the Link tutor involving individual action planning and target setting.

2 Continuity of Professional Development
Individual action planning and associated target setting have become an important part of the Leicester training. They involve negotiation by the student teacher with tutors and peers in the University, and likewise with teaching colleagues and peers in school. Given that one of the principles of Partnership is addressing continuity of professional development, from ITE through the early years in the profession to positions of responsibility in a school, the process of target setting underlies these assumptions of Partnership. Not only is individual action planning a natural extension of this work, it also mirrors such work with pupils and students in many schools and colleges in which they are encouraged to take greater responsibility for recording their own achievements, and for identifying and negotiating their own future pathways. Student teachers thereby obtained the direct experience of action planning and direct involvement through the tutorial support from their university Link tutor that is needed to make it succeed.

Such an individual action planning approach is particularly appropriate to ITE because of the variety of strengths and experiences which different people bring to the understanding and skills that are needed in a teaching career. It is therefore important to begin what is effectively the planning of further professional development, and to use a process which will be encountered later in appraisal schemes. Student teachers get practice in the articulation of their skills and in identifying in a constructive way areas of specific need. They can set achievable goals and gain practice in listening, clarifying and summarising, giving and receiving feedback, being assertive and so on. Likewise appraisal is involved with the asking of questions, making observations in the classroom and sharing good practice with colleagues.

The University was successful in the summer of 1991 in gaining funding from TEED (Training, Enterprise and Education Directorate) administered by the Department of Employment, to support the introduction of Individual Action Planning in teacher training, a major part of which was in ITE. The project as a whole was led by David Tomley, and it released funds to support all Link tutors in their tutorial work with student teachers and their target-setting on the ten professional topics, and to support new initiatives to do with action planning in different subject areas. Such development work included working groups of teachers as well as university tutors, and led to exploratory work in the use of individual action plans with student teachers on block teaching practice, as well as in other parts of the PGCE year. One outcome of the project was to introduce the National Record of Achievement (NRA) to student teachers, and to engage in its use during a first year of teaching those who continued to work within the Leicestershire Education Authority as Newly Qualified Teachers.

3 Teacher Involvement in ITE and University Tutor Involvement in Schools

Partnership provided for joint planning, joint evaluation and, indeed, created opportunities for curriculum development for all the institutions concerned. The overall aim of the university/school Partnership model was one which provided benefits, in terms of professional development, to all participants: student teachers, qualified teachers and university tutors. Certainly Partnership demonstrated ways in which improved ITE for trainees could go hand-in-hand with authentic professional development for teachers and could contribute to a school's programme of curriculum review and classroom evaluation.

The benefits to be derived from these working principles are important to note, before I move on to consider the impact of the more recent and enforced changes in ITE provision.

For the university tutor – with either hat on as subject tutor or as Professional Course Link tutor – there was close and sustained contact with a cluster of schools which provided recent and relevant experience of the whole school issues. Provision was also there for recent and relevant experience of current practice in a specific subject area. This led to the possibility of developing parts of the PGCE course in response to developments in schools. There might also, in the long term, be a place for the university tutor in the delivery of aspects of necessary professional skills through structured INSET in particular schools. Indeed several of us had already contributed to 'in-house' sessions on appraisal, on the use of Information Technology and so on, some of which arose directly out of work done in school with student teachers.

For the school Professional tutor contacts with student teachers and their collaborative project work provided opportunities for the identification of specific curriculum and staff development needs in certain subject areas, or broader areas of concern to the whole school. There was regular contact too with other Professional tutors and the university Link tutor, increasing awareness of the work of a wide variety of staff. Finally, through overall involvement in the Partnership, there was professional development in terms of co-ordination, management and interpersonal skills.

For the school co-tutors there was the chance to explore evaluation techniques which could be linked to research into subject issues, or linked to work with subject departments in other schools, perhaps including those within the same cluster. There was a chance to explore the relationship between subject area and the whole curriculum and, through overall involvement, an opportunity to develop management, interpersonal and tutorial skills.

As university tutors we were relying on co-tutors to help identify in the student teachers any weaknesses or gaps in subject knowledge, and to find ways of supporting specific subject needs. There now exist elsewhere many lists of the possible roles and responsibilities of a subject co-tutor. In 1992 I drew up the following list of roles for a science co-tutor, which I give here by way of – admittedly subject specific – example:

1   Provision of a good role model of teaching in that subject area.
2   Guiding/counselling/advising/coaching/assisting the student teacher with planning a way through a structured PGCE course.
3   Supporting (either directly or indirectly) the collaborative science project.
4   Monitoring and helping with the assessment of teaching practice.
5   Being a source of information about subject content, teaching methodology and school procedures.
6   Providing a good departmental model with schemes of work for the National Curriculum, and providing access to a range of pupils and resources.
7   Removing any constraints and negotiating on behalf of the student teachers with other colleagues in the department.
8   Interpreting the CATE competences so they make sense to science student teachers.

Of more concern was the apparent sheer diversity of experience on offer for the science student teachers in the thirty-five different schools. This in turn raised questions about the necessary range of skills that are needed to be an effective co-tutor in any subject area. It could be a daunting list, and is one in which there are clearly tensions, e.g. the conflicting roles of 'supporter and enabler' and that of 'supervisor and assessor'. In addition I believe there are tensions surrounding existing national programmes of school tutor training. These can assume the passive reception of the necessary skills, based on a model of training which assumes teachers can indeed 'be developed'. School tutor training within a Partnership, on the other hand, is quite clearly an active process. It is about offering teachers, and indeed all participants, an opportunity to develop a broad range of professional skills.

Transfer of Responsibilities 1992–94

In an era of enforced compliance with the law, contracts and agreements between schools and university have had to be made, roles and responsibilities have had to be clarified, job specifications have had to be drawn up for teachers in individual schools, and overall there have been enormous expenditures of time and energy committed to unravelling the funding arrangements, establishing lines of communication and arranging for the transfer of responsibility for parts of the course. The shift to make 66 per cent of the PGCE course school-based did not present a problem and, overall, the structural rearrangements to the school- and university-based components of the PGCE course remain much the same as before. However, not only do the teachers in schools now need to know for what and to whom they are accountable in terms of responsibility for ITE, but the student teachers, too, have an entitlement to minimum levels of support and opportunity in schools. Prior to these new arrangements there had existed only descriptive statements of individual roles, and there could be no insistence that any or part of the descriptive guidelines would be performed. Certainly those ad-hoc arrangements – largely dependent on informal channels of communication – could not and would not have continued.

In some ways the forced changes have produced a greater sense of partnership, most particularly amongst the elected representatives on the Partnership Steering Committee. There is a more realistic and well-developed sense of each other's positions, propelled more quickly to this point as a result of the government initiative. Nevertheless there remains a tight-rope to be walked if the university department is to remain viable in ITE. Further details of the Leicester funding arrangements can be found in Aplin (1994). The financial difficulties, and all the partners' desire to maintain quality in teacher training, have resulted in a two-phase introduction of the necessary changes. Ideally, for such planned development, pilot phases should have accompanied each of the transitions outlined below. Indeed these were originally built into an institutional development plan (May 1993). The enforced time scales have not allowed for this, and so the very necessary exploration of the proposed Records of Personal Development – profiles which might take account of personal qualities and teaching effectiveness, as well as minimal levels of competence – have not been possible, even though we know that any planned developments need to take account of particular contexts and circumstances. No pilot work on monitoring or assessment has been possible in individual subject areas or during block teaching practice.

The introduction of Individual Action Planning (IAP) has had a very large impact on the overall working of the course and its development in keeping in line with requirements of Circular 9/92. The IAP process is central to the student teachers' experience of the course, and has been adapted to the new requirements involving teachers in course design and planning, and the future adoption of a competence-based model of training and assessment. There remain tensions between training for skills competence and exploratory developmental performance; and these are tensions which are difficult to reconcile. There remains also an ignorance of how teachers learn and practise professional skills (skills which incorporate all the class management skills).

In 1994–95 phase one of the transition is being put into place, with schools carrying the responsibility for the monitoring and assessment of 9/92 competence 2.6 (Further Professional Development), and for supervising the student teachers during their school-based subject work. A designated ITT Co-ordinator in each school has assumed the responsibilities once held by the university Link tutors in:

- providing the tutorial support for IAP on these wider professional issues;
- providing student teachers with opportunities for school-based investigations;
- providing support in using resources in school for these investigations;
- assessing the student teachers' competences with respect to competence 2.6.

There is an annual programme of school tutor training to support this transition, and currently many questions are being raised by ITT co-ordinators about the mode of assessment and the definition of minimal levels of competence in this area of Further Professional Development. In addition a great deal of university tutor time has been invested in the development of self-study packs (Professional Development Pack and Subject Development Pack) for supporting the work of student teachers in both professional and subject areas of their work.

The components of assessment of 9/92 competence 2.6 require student teachers to provide:

- Collated evidence relating to the four topics of the Professional Development Pack (PDP). Such evidence is derived from the activities and reading in the pack and elsewhere; it is recorded on summary sheets and kept in a Record of Professional Development.
- A detailed, school-based investigation with a written report (2,000 words) on one topic, with an optional oral presentation.
- Oral evidence of awareness of professional issues during the four IAP tutorials.

- General feedback, e.g. as a result of student group seminars and other professional meetings.

The four Professional topics are derived from the original ten-topic pack, and encompass the following areas:

- Your Roles and Responsibilities as a Teacher.
- Promoting Equal Opportunities for all Learners.
- The School and the Community.
- Secondary Education in England and Wales.

What constitutes 'acceptable evidence' is documented within an ITT co-ordinator's handbook. A range of five categories are given including action research, reviews and personal survey work. Each of the four topic areas requires five items of evidence, covering three types of acceptable evidence. Time will tell if this structure – designed to involve the co-ordinators in a manageable supervisory and assessment task – is acceptable to all concerned.

In 1995–96 phase two of the transition will take place. At the time of writing the Partnership Steering Committee has yet to agree to the division of responsibilities between school and university, and it is likely that the delegation and acceptance of the prescribed roles and responsibilities of the subject co-tutor will be more problematic than those prescribed for the ITT co-ordinator.

We have moved a long way from a genuine partnership based on confidence, trust, shared experiences and distinctive local features. For example, it is more difficult now, as funds transfer to individual schools, to hope that schools will continue to work in the geographical clusters established in the pilot phase of Partnership. In more optimistic moments it is possible to believe such initiatives might flourish; in reality the management of Partnership seems to raise questions which have less to do with the impact of student teachers on the classroom or on pupils' learning.

So can the three principles of partnership, outlined earlier in this chapter, be maintained? It is likely that the opportunity to make subject links with the wider teaching role can continue, though the breadth of experience will be curtailed by the reduced contact with other schools in a cluster. Further development of study materials to be used in subject areas will support student teacher learning, as will the proposed use of individual action planning with subject co-tutors. There is no doubt that the continuity of professional development can be pursued through the use of target setting and tutorial support in both school and university. However, the involvement of the university tutor in school during ITE will be greatly diminished. Already university tutors no longer operate as Link tutors on professional issues in school and it is hard to imagine how the benefits derived from active collaboration in the classroom can be replaced, when the university tutor's role in school is likely to become largely one of monitoring standards and training co-tutors.

In conclusion,

It may be reasonably said then that in the matter of ensuring effective educational change, the education of teachers is a strategic point in the educational system – a point of either strength or weakness. To make it one of the strongest elements must be the aim.

(Simon, 1980, p. 87)

If Partnership is to remain an active process – one of offering teachers, tutors and student teachers a broad range of professional skills – then we should not accept the loss of quality training, and we should continue to put into place only those structures which will minimise the likely reduction in quality.

4

PARTNERSHIP WITH SMALL PRIMARY SCHOOLS

Susan E. Sanders

INTRODUCTION

The recent surge in writing about partnership between schools and Higher Education Institutions (HEI) in the preparation of teachers has until recently been focused on the secondary school (Furlong, Wilkin and Booth, 1990; Shaw, 1992, etc.). The publication of the new regulations for the training of teachers for the primary phase (Welsh Office, WO 1993; DFE, 1993), has heralded the arrival of publications addressing issues in primary schools (Yeomans and Sampson, 1994; Furlong and Maynard, 1995). However, the size of the primary school is not discussed.

This is an important oversight for four reasons.

1. Much that we know about partnership has been learnt from the secondary phase. The partnerships devised in the secondary phase rely in many aspects on a level of staffing and availability of classes not found in schools of less than 150 pupils. The extremes found in small school organisation can force creative planning which can be of use across the primary phase.
2. In 1994 in England[1] 14.6 per cent of our pupils were taught in schools smaller than this (precise figures for Wales not currently available). If such schools are not used, not only are students not afforded the opportunity to work with pupils from the full range of backgrounds, but also pupils are denied the advantages that a good student can give. (Of course they are also denied the disadvantages that a weak student can create!)
3. Not to involve such schools limits the experience of our teachers in training in the main to the urban conurbations. This may lead many to not consider a career in small schools and thus lead to staffing problems in the future. It also limits the experiences of schools, teachers and pupils available for discussion and comparison between students.

4. Many aspects of partnership involve the staff of the school in the role of mentor. This not only includes individual teachers working with individual students in their classrooms, but a senior mentor or professional tutor who takes responsibility for this aspect of a school's work. If staff in small schools do not have the same opportunities to develop these skills as colleagues in larger schools their professional development is limited and future career prospects may suffer.

In this chapter I intend to argue not only for the inclusion of small schools in partnership but to dispel some of the myths that have led to their exclusion and to indicate the strengths of small schools that are invaluable in the training process.

I also suggest some strategies for overcoming some logistical difficulties in the placing of students in small schools.

The writing of this chapter is informed both by my work in initial training and my involvement with two funded research projects into the role of mentoring in primary schools. One research group included two small schools, Helyg Primary School located on the edge of a small village at the end of a valley some 6 miles from the nearest conurbation and Deri Primary School located within a small city.

SMALL PRIMARY SCHOOLS

Each Local Education Authority (LEA) will have its own definition of what makes a primary school small. In 1985 West Glamorgan's Primary Curriculum Working Group designated as small any school whose headteacher had a 'full-time' teaching commitment and up to 130 pupils. Other definitions have ranged from 100 (DES, Gittins, 1967; DES, Plowden, 1967) to 266 (Howells, 1982). For the purposes of this chapter I have taken the idea of any school with less than six teachers (including the headteacher). Within this category some schools may only have one teacher but most will have four or more.

This definition is based on the University of Aston in Birmingham's 1981 notion of a school in which children of more than one age group are placed in every class as a matter of necessity. It also reflects schools in which teachers would have a minimum of two areas of curriculum responsibility each, which I believe has an influence on the time and energy available for other initiatives. Headteachers in such schools are likely to have more extensive teaching commitments than their colleagues in larger schools; although since Local Management of Schools (LMS) they will have more autonomy over staffing decisions.

Small primary schools have been the subject of research including that by Bell and Sigworth, 1987; Barnes and Shinn-Taylor, 1988; Galton and Patrick, 1990; Lewis, 1991; and Keast 1991. None of these have the role of the school in initial teacher training as the major focus. In fact in work such as that of Lewis (1991), which explored the role of the headteacher, involvement with student teachers did not feature at all in their concerns or day-to-day work. However, their findings provide a useful basis for this discussion as they address issues which influence both the decisions of the schools themselves and the HEIs to be involved in partnership.

SMALL PRIMARY SCHOOLS AND INITIAL TEACHER TRAINING

Typically small primary schools have not been involved in all teacher preparation programmes. However, over 30 per cent of primary schools in England in 1994, and between 33 per cent and 44 per cent in Wales in 1993 had less than 150 pupils on role (DFE, 1994). The reasons given by headteachers and HEIs for not involving small schools include accessibility, efficiency, flexibility and organizational matters.

Accessibility and Efficiency

Many HEIs are based in large cities which do not have small schools, e.g. Birmingham, London. Even where HEIs are in smaller cities and towns surrounded by small schools, e.g. Swansea, Lincoln, Norwich, the geographical isolation of the smaller schools has not made it easy to include them in the programme. Even when institutions are placed within an area typified by small schools, e.g. Carmarthen, other considerations have limited their use.

Traditionally students are supported through their time in school by a college-based tutor. Tutors often have limited time in which to make their visits and so accessibility to more than one student per day is important. Institutions prefer to place more than one student in a school for both this reason and to alleviate the isolation that could be felt by a single student.

Flexibility and Organisational Matters

With the smaller number of classes there is less choice of a base class for a student teacher. Two students in a school could mean that every class has a student. Whilst it would be pleasing to imagine that every teacher in every school welcomes the idea of having a student for a period of time, experience tells that this is not the case.

> Student teachers take up too much time . . . We're not here to train teachers . . . It's all too disruptive . . . What will parents think?
> (Reported in Watkins and Whalley, 1993, p. 133)

At the end of the day we are here to teach children and anything else detracts from the classroom planning and teaching so if you've got a student ... I know that teachers in the last two or three years have said to me that whereas before it was a reward having a student after so many years of teaching ... do I have to have a student ... I can't afford the time.

(Mr Babbage, Headteacher, Deri Primary School)

Hence headteachers make careful judgements as to with whom to place a student teacher. The smaller number of teachers in a small school leaves them little flexibility. The effect of an unexpected illness or new member of staff on choice is felt in all schools but is even greater in small schools.

In small schools students are faced with classes with more than one age of pupil (University of Aston, 1981). This is seen as more challenging than single-age classes and hence not the ideal placement for a beginning teacher.

Phil (the new deputy head) has found the mixed-aged class a real challenge and he is an excellent and experienced teacher, so students would find it really difficult.

(Mrs Law, Headteacher, Helyg Primary School)

However, some small schools see the presence of students in such classes as advantageous.

Considerations for Schools Entering Partnership

Watkins and Whalley (1993), whilst writing about the mentoring of beginner teachers, highlight seven issues which schools need to examine as they prepare to be involved in the mentoring elements of partnership. These are:

1. Whole school issues such as ethos, degree of connectedness, view of professional development.
2. Communication issues.
3. Challenges and conflicts such as disruption to pupils, challenging practice.
4. Resources, including time and space.
5. Management of the learning experience to include a range of models, breadth of experience and appropriate support.
6. The number of people involved in the mentoring process.
7. The schools' learning from the process (often expressed as 'what's in it for us?'!).

In the next section I shall examine each of these from the perspective of small schools.

SMALL PRIMARY SCHOOLS AND PARTNERSHIP

Galton and Patrick (1990) undertook research (PRISMS project) in sixty-eight small schools between 1983 and 1985 to examine curriculum provision. The schools in their sample ranged from 16-pupil to 132-pupil schools, which places them within the range of my working definition. Whilst the focus of their research was to identify factors which might limit small schools from delivering the curriculum to their pupils, the three factors they identified as being related to school size can also be seen as influential in the teacher preparation process. These three factors were:

- the smaller professional community immediately available to the teachers for consultation and support;
- the number of adults available to share the work
- the physical constraints of the size of the school.

These factors, and other findings reported by Galton and Patrick (1990), mesh neatly with Watkins and Whalley's issues for schools involved in partnership and provide a basis for the rest of this section.

For the purposes of this chapter I have collapsed Watkins and Whalley's issues into the following four issues which I see as particular to the small school situation. These are: the provision of a wide range of role models and experiences; resources including space, time and people; communication; and management issues such as connectedness, challenges and conflicts. Secondary considerations such as outcomes for the school are also addressed.

PROVISION OF A RANGE OF ROLE MODELS AND EXPERIENCES

Despite some images of the small school as a backwater staffed by dedicated but out of touch older teachers, research shows that in many ways teachers in small schools are exceptional. Galton and Patrick (1990) found that whilst the teachers in their sample were slightly older than the national population of primary teachers, the headteachers were younger and likely to be in their first headship, as were both Mrs Law, Headteacher of Helyg Primary School and Mr Babbage, Headteacher of Deri Primary School. The teachers were also slightly more likely to be graduates. More significantly for involvement in Initial Teacher Training (ITT) they were

> more likely to have taught in four or more schools, to have taught in a greater range of schools of different sizes, to have taught both infants and junior age pupils and to have taught vertically grouped classes.
>
> (Patrick, 1991, p. 60)

By comparing the teachers in their sample with the national population of primary teachers in 1984 (DES, no date; Wragge, Bennett and Carre, 1989) Galton and Patrick concluded that there was no reason why teachers in small schools were any less able to deliver a broad and balanced curriculum than their colleagues in larger schools. Neither did their data suggest that pre-National Curriculum there was anything different about the curriculum provision in small schools.

Teachers in small schools often claim to be professionally isolated (Keast, 1991) and this notion was reinforced by the following anecdote.

> When there were more advisers around . . . they kept more to their Bayside and East Dock schools . . . I know Charles (the previous headteacher) felt it here because he didn't see anybody for the three years he was here!
>
> (Mrs Law, Headteacher, Helyg Primary School)

However, Patrick (1991) suggests that this was a potential isolation rather than one that happened in reality. Certainly evidence exists to support this in recent years. Widespread INSET provision, particularly in connection with the implementation of the National Curriculum orders and assessment procedures (Cox and Sanders, 1994), as well as 'cluster arrangements' (Potter and Williams, 1994), have most probably contributed to the alleviation of previous isolation or self-exclusion. In fact Galton and Patrick (1990) found evidence that the teachers in small schools in their sample were

> just as likely to observe each other at work, and to receive visits from local inspectors or advisors as were their colleagues in the random sample of schools, and they were more likely to work with peripatetic teachers.
>
> (Patrick, 1991, pp. 61–2)

However the perceptions of the teachers are important. Teachers in the Galton and Patrick sample certainly reported that they had little opportunity to make contact with other teachers. Mrs Law reported that LEA inspectors in the past had 'seldom made it up the valley'. Mr Babbage, whose school was within the urban area, did not express such views so geographical isolation may have played a part.

AVAILABILITY OF RESOURCES

About half of Galton and Patrick's (1990) teachers in small schools felt their teaching to be restricted by lack of resources and space. However, this view is not unique to teachers in small schools. Teachers interviewed as part of research into the implementation of the National Curriculum (Cox and Sanders, 1994) listed lack of resources including time as one of the limiting factors. Schools involved in our ITT course informally reporting cramped classrooms and staffrooms, and no spare rooms available to tutors for consultation, include those with upwards of 400 pupils.

COMMUNICATION

Watkins and Whalley (1993) discuss the several aspects of communication that affect the effectiveness of a partnership programme. The HEI and the school, the HEI and the students, the school and the students, and the staff within the school must all have efficient lines of communication if the partnership is to succeed. Some of these are liable to be influenced by the size of the school. Care must be taken not to assume that some of the characteristics described as advantageous by headteachers are in fact so. A school with a small number of staff may perceive lines of communication between those staff as simply informal.

> One can tend to feel rather comfortable in its closeness and its smallness. But what I feel is that although it's small you need formal meetings. You need to have minutes taken, you need to have an agenda, because although we're only five staff there is a time when someone might say 'I didn't know that,' 'ah yes, but I've got the minutes'. We can become too comfortable in our situation and think that everybody is taking everything in . . .'
>
> (Mrs Law, Headteacher, Helyg Primary School)

With a smaller number of staff involved, the possibility of the students getting 'mixed messages' about school policy, rules and rituals should be diminished. However, the production of supporting materials for the students, and their induction into the school life, will have to be undertaken as yet another task by a teacher already responsible for two, three or more aspects of school life, whereas in a larger school a member of staff may be identified to undertake this as their primary or secondary role.

For example, the headteacher of a twelve-teacher school reported that:

> I've created a special post, with an incentive point, for responsibility for students and new teachers.
>
> (Mr Edwards, Headteacher, Ysgol Maes-yr-Haf)

Whereas the headteacher of a six-teacher school reported:

> I've done a good deal of the work on the file for students and new teachers myself, because I really didn't feel that I could ask any of the staff to do anything else at the moment.

> If I could say to Mrs White, or to any other member of staff, you have no curriculum responsibilities this year, we are having so many students in, this will be . . . your job for the year, then fine. Then they can forget the curriculum areas, but when they've got language, things to do with policies, schemes of work and all that, that's the problem.
>
> (Mr Babbage, Headteacher, Deri Primary School)

MANAGEMENT ISSUES SUCH AS CONNECTEDNESS, CHALLENGES AND CONFLICTS

As Watkins and Whalley point out

> Significant learning is likely to be challenging, as enquiry into areas of teaching and school life is not always comfortable. The presence of a beginner teacher can highlight issues in the organisation, and examining procedures and practice may trigger a range of reactions causing anxiety and at worst polarisation.
>
> (Watkins and Whalley, 1993, p. 132)

Small primary schools are no less vulnerable to this than large schools. However, because of their size in order to survive they will have been forced to work through and thus dissipate polarisation.

> It could be more difficult in a small school than in a large school if you had clashes of personality, non-communication between staff. I've seen that ... The way we worked round that ... together with my nursery nurse we came in in the morning and made everybody a cup of tea ... The tea's in the staff room and it gets people together.
>
> (Mrs Law, Headteacher, Helyg Primary School)

Watkins and Whalley also warn against interpersonal conflicts and, whereas in a larger school students have a wider choice from which to find a kindred spirit or to go elsewhere for support, this will not be the case in a small school. Neither is there as much flexibility in placement if a relationship goes disastrously wrong. However, part of the role of the school is to induct the student into the profession, and an important part of that learning is to learn to work with colleagues of differing views. The smaller school forces the student to undertake this learning in a way that larger schools may not. Large schools may also have divisive cliques and groupings which do not necessarily provide good role models for the student. Both Mrs Law and Mr Babbage felt that this was much less likely to happen in small schools. There are simply not enough people for it to happen. However, there can be an overpowering cohesiveness that isolates the newcomer, and small schools and HEIs entering into partnership should address this issue. Mrs Law felt that the placement of more mature students in Helyg Primary School meant that they were more able to cope with being the only student in the school as they had commonalities with the staff that very young students would not.

Watkins and Whalley highlight the importance of a connectedness between the staff, and most teachers who were interviewed for the PRISMs project reported liking being involved in so many aspects of school life. In a small school the connectedness is apparent, everyone is involved in many aspects of the school's life.

OUTCOMES FOR THE SCHOOL

For the small school one of the perceived outcomes of involvement in ITT is definitely access to a broader professional community. The students and HEI tutors bring different ideas, subject expertise and connections to the smaller school. As Mrs Law said, 'I do think it's important for a small school with a small staff to widen their horizons.'

For the pupils it is an opportunity to chose from a broader range of role models including contrasting ages, genders, cultural backgrounds and interests. Whilst this may also be true in larger schools it is particularly apparent in smaller schools.

ADVANTAGES OF SMALL SIZE

To summarize, the advantages of the small school as a partner in a teacher preparation programme rest on its connectedness and the accessibility of all staff. The ethos of the small school often includes elements of care and support that are crucial to learning teachers. However, there are dangers of claustrophobia, lack of peers and outsiderness that must be carefully addressed and are not unique to the small school.

SOME STRATEGIES FOR SMALL PRIMARY SCHOOLS IN PARTNERSHIP

Small schools are often keen to be involved in the ITT partnership. In order to facilitate such partnerships the following strategies are offered to relieve the tensions articulated by both schools and HEIs, i.e. overburdening of staff (with no tangible reward) and the perceived narrowness of experience.

Working in More than One School

In many areas small schools are already linked through cluster or grouping arrangements. (Cave and Cave, 1982; Fitzgerald, 1984; Bayliss, 1985). By using such arrangements small schools can provide a wider experience for students by simply including them in cluster activities or by organising teaching experience in more than one school. Shaw (1992) argues for this in connection with much larger secondary schools. Mrs Law could see the potential for having one mentor amongst a cluster of schools, thus alleviating some pressure on staff.

Changing the Style of Teaching Practice

Small schools can also offer multiple places for students by moving away from the one student, one teacher, one classroom model and having team teaching approaches. Such approaches have been used quite successfully in the secondary school partnership programmes involving my own institution.

Financial Arrangements

As mentioned earlier some schools have created specific posts for the senior mentor. If this is accompanied by financial or other rewards the post is enhanced in the staff's eyes. HEIs should be creative with the arrangements of payments to schools. When a sum of money follows each student, schools that are able to take larger numbers of students can accrue moneys to facilitate such 'sweeteners'. A school that can only take one or two students will not be so fortunate. HEIs could choose to pay a lump sum to each school that is in partnership and supplement that with a smaller sum per student.

Beyond the Teaching Practice

The partnership need not focus only on the assessed teaching practice. Non-assessed work that focuses early in the course on working alongside teachers to learn about classroom organisation, questioning techniques etc., or work later in the course that focuses on specific curriculum areas such as IT or issues such as stereotyping, can be organised in and benefit smaller schools.

This year we are developing our school-based programme. As well as addressing the requirements of the new regulations (WO, 1993; DFE, 1993) we are intending to involve as many small schools as possible. This year our autumn term programme has included five single and five consecutive days placement in a school for groups of students. During this time students have been undertaking tasks in school on general aspects such as classroom management, planning and pupils with special needs as well as tasks connected with the teaching of the core subjects. The senior mentor has been responsible for managing the programme within the school, and providing seminar and tutorial support. The honorarium paid to schools has not been dependent on the numbers of students that the school has taken and we have managed to include four small schools within the twenty-two schools that have been involved.

CONCLUSION

I have argued in the early part of this chapter that many of the reasons why some small schools exclude themselves and why HEIs may be reluctant to consider small schools for partnership are not supported by research. I believe that it is important to form partnerships between small schools and HEIs as part of teacher preparation programmes because not to do so:

• limits the students' experiences of organisation, locale and a true overview of our education system;
• deprives teachers and pupils in small schools of opportunities afforded to those in larger schools;
• and also deprives students of the opportunity to consider such schools as part of their future careers.

I also believe that, whilst not unique to small schools, their close-knit nature and connectedness facilitate a whole school approach and a supportive environment in which our student teachers can learn. Much of this is of a speculative nature and needs to be researched more extensively. For this to happen colleagues in both small schools and HEIs will have to form partnerships. I hope this chapter will have at least encouraged them to consider the possibility.

NOTES

1. This figure was kindly provided by John Bamber of the DFE Analytical Services Branch (DFE, 1994). The Education Statistics for the United Kingdom (Government Statistical Services, 1994) publish the following categories: less than 25, 26 to 50, 51 to 100, 100 to 200 and so on.

5

OPEN LEARNING AND THE PGCE: A PRIMARY EXPERIENCE

Jill Bourne and Jenny Leach

The development of a new Open University PGCE has been coincidental with, although certainly facilitated by, the government's thrust towards school-based teacher training in the 1990s. As Furlong *et al.* (1988) have argued, there were a variety of motives behind changes in teacher education over the last decade, besides the most obvious ones of government policy. The aim of the OU PGCE as outlined in the 1992 *Statement of Aims* is to 'extend access to the teaching profession through a part-time, multimedia course which will be organised in partnership with schools'. Initial research undertaken by the OU in the late 1980s under the direction of Bob Moon found a substantial interest in an OU part-time PGCE among many undergraduates taking OU courses. Many of those expressing interest were qualifying in mathematics and science, both 'shortage subjects'. The OU was soon afterwards granted around £2m. by the DES to develop an open learning course to begin in February 1994, preparing students for teaching at either primary or secondary level across a range of subject specialisms.

OPEN LEARNING AND THE PGCE

The OU PGCE is an eighteen-month long, part-time course, divided into three stages. One full-time block school placement is required in each stage of the course, with two weeks minimum to be undertaken in a second school, and with an additional three weeks equivalent to be spent in school across the period of the course, giving eighteen weeks of school-based study in total.

Each student on the OU PGCE course is provided with a range of resources

APPENDIX 1A

COURSE OUTLINE FOR PRIMARY COURSES

			Study time	School placements*	
STAGE 1	BLOCK 1	Introduction	20 hours		Feb
	BLOCK 2	Stage 1 curriculum studies and application	55 hours	3 weeks full-time	March
STAGE 2	BLOCKS 3 & 4	Stage 2 curriculum studies and application	180 hours		April
		Focus on:			May
		curriculum planning, organisation, management and assessment;			June
		the development of teaching and learning within the primary classroom;			July
		English, mathematics, science, RE and PE within the primary curriculum.			Aug
					Sept
				4 weeks full-time	Oct
					Nov
STAGE 3	BLOCK 5	Part A: Language and learning	120 hours		Dec
		Part B: Learning for all			Jan
		Part C: Effective schools			
		Part D: Curriculum studies and application			Feb
	BLOCK 6	Stage 3 curriculum studies and application	120 hours		March
		Focus on:			
		further development of all aspects introduced in Stage 2;			April
		the teaching of national curriculum foundation subjects.		8 weeks full-time	May
					June
	BLOCK 7	Preparation for induction and further professional development	10 hours		July

* Involvement in school-based activities across the 18 months, (e.g. parents evenings, drama, music, sports) 3 weeks

Figure 5.1.

to support their learning, including study guides, resource packs, school experience guides, video and audio materials, and the loan of a personal computer complete with modem and software. A key resource is the *PGCE Study Guide*, which integrates the course, directing students from readings to videos and audio cassettes, and calling for reflection on school experience.

The *School Experience Guide* is a second key element in the course. It structures school placements for all students through a staged range of directed activities in school, designed for progression in teaching competence and the development of professional values. In this way it offers the basic 'entitlement' which each student can expect from their school placement. It is an element in the OU quality assurance system, ensuring basic comparability in experience for all our students.

The course operates on the premise that within the structured and supportive framework we provide for them our students, as mature and independent adults intending to become professionals, should be expected to organise their work programme, manage their time, negotiate working relationships with mentors and other school staff and keep clear records of work. We wanted to set up systems which treat students as partners with the university and the schools in their own professional development. Later in this chapter we will illustrate how these expectations are working out in practice.

A NEW SOCIAL GEOGRAPHY OF TEACHER EDUCATION

Andy Hargreaves (1995) has drawn attention to the ways in which teacher education is being radically transformed as the century draws to a close, most particularly in its 'social geography'. Teacher education is rapidly being deinstitutionalised and, as he puts it, 're-embedded in other sites and spaces'. Rather than being contained within a limited number of teacher education institutions, it is becoming dispersed across a variety of schools and school clusters. This dispersal can be seen more generally in the way information is disseminated, especially in the IT explosion with its array of options from satellite or cable tv, the rapid growth of the internet, and the increasing ability to access libraries and resources from a remote terminal. In this context images of open learning do not seem so revolutionary: OU PGCE students working from their kitchen table or sitting room, analysing practice on a video from Northern Ireland, Tower Hamlets or Devon, and logging on to their computers to join a conference via electronic mail with fellow students and tutors across the UK. Indeed it seems a perfectly feasible way to study and, while not to every student's taste, an important way of giving access to teacher education for those who for one reason or another find it difficult to reach a more conventional course or to study within institutional hours.

However, rather than the dispersal of students, it is another kind of dispersal, that of the shift of responsibilities for teacher development and assessment to schools, which Hargreaves suggests many teacher educators find threatening. He sees two ways forward: one is to choose to create small, special and protected places, 'professional development schools', in which to maintain and develop an elite form of teacher education; the second is to look for new ways of working across dispersed sites in ways which will enhance learning for all concerned.

Both options, Hargreaves suggests, have problems. The first option may maintain islands of calm and a sense of professional identity, but may bear little relation to the situations in which students leaving the institution will then find themselves: 'Professional development schools are . . . tiny, tidier versions of the educationally messy worlds they stylishly misrepresent' (Hargreaves, forthcoming p. 28). The second option, dispersing teacher education across multiple small sites, has the danger of hiding its consequences. As Hargreaves points out it may become 'everywhere and nowhere', and thus unaccountable; it may also narrow horizons, just reproducing existing practice, rather than challenging and changing it.

In designing the Open University PGCE we have taken the second option; we have accepted and even embraced the opportunity to work across multiple school sites and very different contexts. However, we have also tried to develop systems which avoid the dangers Hargreaves identifies: by setting up quality assurance systems to make our practice as accountable and open as possible, and combating the danger of narrow horizons for students through the variety of practice we share with them.

If we can get the system right we should ensure the support necessary to make most schools places which can competently prepare people for the realities of schooling while at the same time, with the help of the course materials, providing them with 'a conceptual and attitudinal basis for coping with and seeking to alter those realities' in order to improve learning (Sarason, 1993). In the remainder of this paper, then, we will describe how we have tried to respond to the challenge of large scale, dispersed teacher education.

A REGIONAL SUPPORT STRUCTURE

The key to understanding how the OU PGCE works lies in understanding the partnership between the central course writing team at the OU's campus at Milton Keynes and the School of Education's regional staff. Although a national programme, the OU PGCE is administered on a day-to-day basis by academic staff located in twelve regional offices across England, Wales and Northern Ireland. These regional staff, known as staff tutors, with the support of the central writing team, are responsible for appointing and training local part-time OU tutors for the course, developing contacts with schools, monitoring the interviewing and selection of students by schools, organising mentor briefings and supporting partner schools, organising day schools and tutorials for students, and (a crucial role) 'troubleshooting' in individual cases as needed.

All the staff tutors, like the central writing team, are qualified teachers, with either HE or local authority advisory service teacher education experience behind them. Regional staff tutors have contributed strongly to the course, many having written sections of the material as well as having provided critical feedback and commentary on drafts. This firm regional presence is a vital part of the OU PGCE.

PARTNERSHIPS WITH SCHOOLS

Schools involved in the OU PGCE can be found across England, Wales and Northern Ireland. Course development from the start was based on work in schools. Primary video and audio materials, for example, draw on rural, suburban and inner-city schools, from Cumbria to Exeter and West Belfast to Newry. Written course modules, too, are built around case studies of classroom practice. Schools have also acted as critical readers of all primary materials. We cannot stress enough how important teachers' willingness to share their practice has been in course development.

However, our 'partner schools' are essentially those schools which, alongside the OU, are implementing the PGCE course for the approximately 1,400 students currently registered for the course and the prospective students already interviewed for the next course cycle. As eighteen-month course cycles overlap, the OU can have up to 3,000 schools involved in the partnership scheme for six months of each year.

Such a large enterprise requires a clear framework of responsibilities and student entitlements, but one within which local strengths must be accommodated. With students so dispersed, school-based programmes clearly cannot be negotiated by the OU school by school. A simple but rigorous framework for assessment is also essential in order to operate across very differing contexts. Although developed in consultation with schools, the responsibility for establishing and monitoring school experience and assessment frameworks has to be taken by the University and responsibility for implementing these accepted by those who wish to be OU partner schools. New partners necessarily enter into an existing framework for school-based study and the development of teaching competences, and accept an assessment framework, which is not open to negotiation as far as the immediate period of that student's PGCE coursework is concerned. At the same time, the frames have to be flexible enough to offer space for local variation, since it is pointless to set conditions which some schools are unable to meet, and unwise to close off opportunities for students to benefit from local strengths.

The OU *Course Handbook for Partner Schools* sets out the basic framework for the PGCE, and explicitly addresses the different roles and responsibilities of the institutions and people involved. The key activities required are summarised as follows. The school:

- 'Agrees, provisionally, to provide a school placement for applicants.
- Interviews the applicant and enters into partnership agreement with the OU.
- Nominates a class teacher as mentor.
- Designates a senior member of staff to (i) liaise with the OU; (ii) play a role in validating teaching assessments.
- Supports the student through three periods of school experience and practice.
- Facilitates access for the student to school-related activities and, when appropriate, opportunities to gain some teaching experience in a second school.
- Participates with University staff in the assessment of the student including the final recommendation to the Assessment Board for the award of Qualified Teacher Status.'

(*Course Handbook for Partner Schools*, OU, 1994)

Open University guidelines are provided for schools to support the initial interviewing process and to ensure equal opportunities are met. OU staff tutors monitor a proportion of all interviews to ensure the guidelines are being followed.

THE MENTOR AND SCHOOL CO-ORDINATOR

The mentor is a key person within the OU scheme. In the majority of cases the primary student will spend most of the block periods of school-based work in the mentor's class. As the course extends over eighteen months this will usually entail working with two different classes of children. The directed activities which we set for students in school, however, require students also to work alongside other teachers in their classes, including the school curriculum leader for the student's own subject specialism. Students also interview senior staff to find out about school-wide policies as well as classroom issues. It is recommended that small rural schools make provision within a 'cluster' of local schools to enable students to have experience of working with an appropriate curriculum subject specialist or with a learning support teacher, for example. The *School Experience Guide* in this way provides both consistency of experience and a tool for negotiating a variety of teaching opportunities.

Every school receives a substantial pack of mentor materials, including videos. The mentor is asked to enable the student to complete the required classroom and school-based activities which are set in the *School Experience Guide*, to provide support for their teaching and feedback on their progress through regular debriefings. The university, in planning the activities, bears in mind the variety of ways in which classrooms are organised, schools are structured, and the curriculum planned across the years. We try to structure activities so that they can be carried out by all students without disrupting the planned work of the class, leaving mentors and students with enough unstructured time to allow the student to play a full part in the life of the school and take advantage of local strengths. This balance of centrally directed activities and those locally negotiated between the student and the school will continue to be tuned and adapted in relation to feedback and monitoring as the course is implemented.

One aspect of partnership which is fundamental to the construction of the course is the practice of co-operative teaching for staff development. The practice of 'co-teaching' classes with the student is an essential part of mentoring for the OU. In this way, through their training, we hope to develop teachers who are willing and enthusiastic about teaching alongside curriculum development leaders, learning support staff, language support teachers and bilingual teachers and assistants.

The mentor does not carry the sole responsibility for partnership with the OU in the school. To support the mentor the partner school also nominates a senior member of staff, called the 'school co-ordinator', who acts as a management link to the university, ensures the student can carry out necessary 'school-wide' activities and validates school-based assessments of the student's progress (see below, p. 65). The school co-ordinator is the person who, should any difficulties emerge, is responsible for contacting the regional OU staff tutor.

THE ROLE OF THE OU TUTOR

In addition to school support an OU part-time tutor/counsellor, each a qualified teacher with recent and relevant experience, is appointed to support every group of fifteen students. The tutor/counsellor is contracted to provide readily accessible personal support for each individual student throughout the course, as well regular group tutorials. While the mentor provides in-depth knowledge of one class in a particular context, and the opportunity for students to observe and discuss practice with an experienced teacher, the role of the tutor complements the mentor's by drawing links in tutorials and in feedback on written assignments between the students' experience in schools and the course materials. This support provides breadth as well as depth of experience, and gives students the opportunity to analyse a range of practice outside the pressures of the school context. Tutors assess four written assignments across the eighteen months, each of these designed to incorporate elements of the directed activities which students carry out in schools.

In regional day schools and tutorials students share experiences and draw support from their peers. In addition each student has access to conferencing facilities on their computer, part of the PGCE resource materials. This allows them greater contact with their tutor and tutor groups, as well as the opportunity to join in wider conferences with other OU PGCE students and staff, including smaller, more 'special interest' conferences on, for example, their specialist subject area or a topic such as intercultural education. (Each computer, its software and modem, will be passed on to the student's placement school after the PGCE course is completed, as part of the OU commitment to partner schools.)

THE PGCE IN PRACTICE

The chapter so far has necessarily focused on the 'enabling level of partnership' (Alexander, 1990), the setting up of systems to facilitate initial teacher education. The 'action level', focusing on 'the day-to-day interactions of the various individuals and groups who operate at the cutting edge of the teacher education process: students, tutors, and the teachers and pupils with whom and in whose classrooms teachers work' (ibid, p. 60) is not yet clear, as the OU PGCE is still new. However, we will *illustrate* the programme at work and some of the issues it has begun to raise in practice, with examples drawn from just one region in the first months of operation.

The East Anglian Region currently supports seventy-two primary and a hundred secondary PGCE students across a large and sprawling region stretching from the outer London boroughs in the south across to The Wash at its most northerly edge, and from the multicultural communities of Luton, Bedford and Peterborough on its westward side to the fenland villages of Cambridgeshire and the hinterland of Suffolk on its eastern perimeter. Its partner schools inevitably vary considerably in character, size and setting. Such differences are reflected in the range of classrooms in the primary course materials.

For those of us employed in the regions to work directly with schools and students on the new PGCE programme, the notion that we would be starting from a blank page in building up partnerships was daunting – but it was a notion that quite quickly proved to be unfounded in several respects. Even before the course started the Open University was approached by many schools whose staff already had a clear understanding of the realities of open learning. These included schools which had used OU courses for staff development; individual teachers studying for an OU MA, or with headteachers themselves Open University graduates. Many schools saw in the Open University scheme an opportunity for staff development and reflection on practice. Many prospective PGCE students already had close relationships with schools, as primary helpers, parents, librarians, or bilingual support teachers.

A minority of prospective students experienced difficulties in finding a partner school to nominate on their application form. This early difficulty is gradually being eased as regions build up closer links with schools. Although students are still encouraged to make their own arrangements, staff tutors play an increasing role in helping to locate suitable schools where students have drawn a blank. Regional staff make use of a growing database of prospective partner schools within the region. It is encouraging that significant numbers of schools involved with the first cohort of students are asking to be included.

When we asked students about their perceptions of the task of finding a partner school themselves, they said that in retrospect they valued the process. Visiting schools and talking to teachers helped confirm in their minds that this was what they really wanted to do. It also helped them to decide which line – upper or lower primary – they would choose.

MENTORS AND STUDENTS IN PARTNERSHIP

In considering the partnership model being developed in the OU it is important to bear in mind that the majority of OU students are mature people who come to the course from a wide variety of employment and life experience. Just 20 per cent of OU PGCE students are under 30 years, compared to 52 per cent under 26 years nationally (DFE, 1992).

Our students have also deliberately chosen a part-time, distance education course. A third of them are OU graduates well used to this method of study. This distinctive student profile challenges Alexander's (1990) assertion that 'it is very easy to forget that [PGCE] students are usually young adults still in the process of establishing their personal identities and independence, frequently insecure and vulnerable.' In fact evidence from PGCE interviews, school reports and feedback from mentors and tutors testify to the very definite expectations, strong motivation to succeed, and high level of personal independence and organisation displayed by OU students. 'Commitment total'; 'perfectionist'; 'total commitment and professional attitude'; 'strong commitment to working with children'; 'showed strong commitment to the course'. These phrases recur throughout the students' school reports.

Whilst this clearly stands many of our students in good stead in schools, there is a small minority of students who need steadying in their extremes of enthusiasm, prolific school experience files and over-zealous questioning of school staff. There are also, of course, many hidden pressures on our students which inform this strong determination to succeed. One such pressure is a product of the fact that 75 per cent are women, many of whom hope to return to paid employment after time at home full-time parenting. In a study of primary students in another OU region Burgess (1994) has noted: 'Throughout all their experiences run threads of endeavour, to successfully perform the dual role of being mother and going out to work.'

So how have students gone about forming partnerships with schools? We will look at two or three brief examples of the process. (The names are of course pseudonyms.)

Case Studies

Elaine's experience is by no means unique within the scheme; she illustrates the mature entrant who is very clear about her goals. Her partnership with a primary school has developed as an almost seamless continuation of her personal and professional life experience. She is 43; an Open University graduate who has recently been working as a voluntary helper in primary classrooms.

> I began my Open University studies in 1989, with the specific aim of entering the teaching profession and have carefully constructed a degree profile with that end in view. My interest in teaching was first aroused some eighteen years ago, when I worked as an assistant in a nursery school . . . I gave this up following the birth of my second child. I feel I have the necessary qualities to make a useful and committed member of the teaching profession.

Elaine approached the school where she had been working – 'not as a parent but on a semi-professional, voluntary basis' – to be her PGCE partner school. It is important to note that the school did not take this decision lightly: 'The head said he would have to be sure about what he was taking on. The school thought long and hard before it decided to commit itself to take me.'

During a successful first school experience Elaine found no difficulty with the transition from helper to student, still finding herself being 'treated as a colleague'. The biggest difficulty she faced in fact was the 'intensive nature of the full-time placement' after part-time work, in particular the demands of having to make detailed classroom observations and the constant reflection on practice. However, she also notes a potential difficulty in working with a known partner: 'There's an element of being grateful to the school, not wanting to make demands on them, "aren't they good to have agreed to have me".'

Yet in the developing relationship between the mentor and student there is a growing recognition on both sides of the additional commitment and responsibilities each brings to the new role. The student comments 'My mentor is excellent. She gives up a lot of her time to support me. I couldn't succeed in the course without her.' In turn the mentor makes use of the term 'partnership' in summarising her evaluation of student progress: 'Elaine was always willing to put in a "full" day. She had looked forward to the three weeks. Her enthusiasm and enjoyment was still there at the end of the school experience. We look forward to continuing this partnership.'

Explicit references to 'partnership' recur throughout the school experience reports. The term is frequently placed alongside the appreciation of the qualities which so many of these mature students bring from previous work experiences. Dilip is a 30-year old history graduate. Before joining the OU PGCE he worked as a teaching assistant for children with special educational needs. Not only does his mentor commend him for being 'keen to learn and enthusiastic', she notes that 'his questioning of staff was relevant'. In common with many other mentors she also includes the importance of relationships with the wider school community, commenting 'he was at ease in the staff room – communicating with teachers, ancillaries and office staff . . . he has made a very good start to his partnership with us.'

Anna is also a mature entrant, a psychology graduate with considerable experience of youth work, having been manager of a youth and community centre. In her application she is clear about the opportunity that the OU course gives her; 'Because of family responsibility and circumstance I can only pursue this [teaching] interest if training can be locally based and this new PGCE course offers such a hope.'

Anna's school is impressed with the high level of her commitment: 'Well motivated . . . keen and enthusiastic about everything she does and this helps her relationship with the children.' But also, as in Dilip's school, the staff value other qualities which her wider experiences contribute to the partnership. 'She is never sparing with her time. She asks many questions but is never intrusive, always aware of other commitments teachers have.'

Many of our students continue to show this commitment to partnership by maintaining links with and contributing to their partner schools between school experiences, going in once or twice a week on a voluntary basis to work with classes or individuals, developing projects they have started or attending INSET days.

In the complex and delicate business of establishing relationships with schools, qualities of commitment, sensitivity, an appreciation of the importance of the wider school community as well as a willingness to contribute to it are all strongly valued. Similarly students value the opportunity that partner schools provide – guided by the OU frameworks and model of mentoring – to be autonomous learners and reflective in their practice. 'Her commitment has been total' comments a mentor. 'She has arrived early and stayed late to prepare and complete work. Each experience has been viewed as a learning platform . . . she has proved to be a reliable and conscientious colleague. She relates well with other members of staff and has assisted with the production of an updated staff handbook.'

NEGOTIATING A WORTHWHILE SCHOOL EXPERIENCE

The *School Experience Guide* acts as a common framework for student and mentor and a guide to entitlement within the OU school experience elements. For Mary its supportive structure was vital when things did not initially go smoothly in her first school experience. Mary is a 33-year-old geography graduate who has worked as a cartographer, public house manager and area sales manager. Before starting the course she wrote: 'My drive and motivation is no longer powered by financial reward alone . . . I personally feel I have a great deal to offer the teaching profession which in turn will give me a second chance at a career that is both rewarding and challenging'.

In common with most OU students Mary selected a local school as her partner school, but not before visiting numerous infant schools in the neighbourhood. This particular school seemed right to her and in turn they accepted her 'because several of the staff were OU students and they agreed with the course. They were very warm, very receptive to the PGCE and very interested to know how it would work.' Mary's own son also became a pupil at the school after she began the course. This was also discussed at her initial interview and was not a problem for either her or the school: 'I am able to separate the two roles.'

In the first week of her first school placement she was disappointed by the help she was receiving. Although keen to support her, the school had no previous experience of students and, despite an initial mentor briefing, Mary's mentor was still having difficulty finding a focus for the placement. The student alerted regional staff to the concern but no intervention was in fact necessary. Using the *School Experience Guide* as a basis for discussion, student, mentor and school co-ordinator were together able to negotiate and plan the experiences the school was required to facilitate. Time was also guaranteed from the second week onwards for mentor and student to meet regularly for planning and evaluation.

Both student and school were pleased with the outcome of this and the subsequent placement. The school report reflects the initiative the student was able to take within the partnership framework.

> She has shown total commitment and a professional attitude in her personal organisation. She showed initiative and proficiency on most activities she undertook and she was never afraid to ask for advice or assistance when needed.

How does Anna, the psychology graduate introduced earlier in this chapter, feel after the second placement?

> It's been very much my initiative. Me leading. The *School Experience Guide* is brilliant. I did keep jumping up and down, my idea was to get this routine, I wanted it to work for others too! There was caution on the staff's part at the beginning, but it's changed now. It was an unknown for both partners, but it's developed well. The school's been interviewing for another student – they obviously think it works!

Anna's additional comments underline the commitment that we have indicated drives so many of our students.

> Students who take this course have to be dedicated, organised and strong willed! It's very easy at the end of the day, when you've been working or being a mum, to say 'I'll sit in front of the telly tonight'. Though

there have been moments when I want to jack it all in, I'm still totally positive.

PROVIDING SUPPORT FOR SCHOOLS

As with any teacher training course, however, things do not always go smoothly in schools. In the best schools mentors fall ill, school co-ordinators are promoted; there are also inevitably a small number of schools which prove unsuitable partners. What are the systems which alert us to difficulties a few students will inevitably encounter?

Staff tutors are responsible for monitoring 15 per cent of school interviews and also for visiting an agreed percentage of schools involved in the programme at each stage. National monitoring is also being carried out by the PGCE Programme Team, and a team of HMI from OFSTED have been inspecting the programme since its inception. They have carried out their own visits to schools and mentors; their report will provide further opportunities to assess how the system is working and to make any necessary adaptations.

In addition to this ongoing quality assurance work, staff tutors are required to visit every student and school where a borderline pass or borderline fail category is indicated in the school placement report. Schools are urged to contact regional staff early on in the placement if a student is experiencing difficulties or if it looks likely that a borderline grade will be given. While such students are in a small minority the cause of problems will vary, ranging from those one or two students who need to be counselled out of the course to those in schools which are themselves failing to provide adequate support and feedback to students.

Apart from formal monitoring requirements staff tutors constantly use informal feedback such as discussion with students over the telephone, and at day schools to be alerted to situations that indicate the potential need for additional monitoring or support – from the student who rings about a late assignment because she has just had a baby, to an overly brief school report that raises cause for concern. Tutor/counsellors pass on concerns about a student to the staff tutor. Similarly at mentor briefings individual concerns raised by mentors can be followed up by telephone or visit. Queries from students or mentors relating to the school experience also act as an impotant alert to a situation where a student may not be receiving full support or where a mentor may need additional help from regional staff in dealing with this vital role.

It can be seen from this outline that the key link person in relation to school and student support is the OU regional staff tutor, who monitors school-based work and student progress in each region, and who undertakes a 'trouble-shooting' role where necessary, mediating between the university, student and school. In the first years of the course, as we clarify and adapt materials both for the schools and for students in the light of experience, the staff tutor is playing an even more central role in ensuring the course is successful.

THE ROLE OF SCHOOL PARTNERS IN ASSESSMENT

The assessment model provides the structure for formative and summative assessment of students' progress. It identifies five broad areas of teaching competence and relates these to a similar number of professional qualities and values. Students themselves, supported by structured course materials, have the responsibility for collecting and presenting evidence that they have demonstrated competence in each of these areas by the end of the course. The assessment model is also used formatively by the mentor, backed by the school co-ordinator, at each stage of the course to structure feedback reports from the school to the university on the student's progress.

Final evidence for assessment consists of the presentation to the university of:

- four tutor-marked assignments based on school experiences;
- evidence, collected and presented by the student, of the completion of a range of directed activities set by the university to show a range of teaching competences and professional qualities;
- three school reports completed by the school within a structured format at the end of each main block placement;
- and a log of additional school experiences verified by the school.

Teacher assessment is complemented by a stringent system of monitoring visits by OU staff, covering a high percentage of schools in the initial years of the programme.

The mentor materials provide detailed guidance for school-based assessments. Support for assessment and moderation is also an important aspect of the regular regional briefings for mentors, held before each block school placement. Early in the programme primary mentors voiced some concern about the assessment aspect of their role. We have seen them gain confidence in this area as they have become more familiar with their student and with the support available from the OU. However, the opportunity to discuss school reports and the assessment framework with fellow mentors in regional briefings seems to have been particularly helpful. We have facilitated developing mentor networks through circulating contact numbers and encouraging voluntary pairings of neighbouring schools.

CONCLUSION

The OU emphasis on observation and co-analysis of teaching between class teacher and PGCE student, on the structured teaching activities required of the PGCE students by the course, the presence of a wide range of OU materials in the school, and the requirements of the assessment framework, appear to us to have a huge in-service potential for schools. Open learning approaches to initial teacher education also provide access to this in-service potential as much in the more remote areas of the country as in better served urban areas. We hope that in addition the electronic mail facilities inherited by the school when each OU student leaves will enable schools to maintain and extend communication networks begun with the PGCE. This offers the prospect of an exciting new 'social geography' of school-based continuing professional development to parallel the expanding possibilities of initial teacher education, which we know we have only just begun to explore.

SECTION THREE

Mentor Development and Support

6

DIAGNOSTIC MONITORING IN A PRIMARY PARTNERSHIP

Lynn D. Newton

INTRODUCTION

Few tutors from HEIs are likely to oppose the principle of partnership in training underlying current changes in teacher education so long as the expertise of both sides in a genuine partnership is recognised. At the University of Newcastle upon Tyne we have moved along this route with postgraduate primary students, with a project called Supporting Student Learning: Practice and Diagnostic Monitoring Project – the Diagnostic Monitoring Project (DMP) for short. This project, its rationale and how it developed, are what I will describe in this chapter.

At Newcastle we have no undergraduate teacher training; we offer only postgraduate courses for prospective primary and secondary teachers. Student numbers are high, usually about 300 or so, of whom about one-third are primary focused. In the early 1990s, in line with other HEIs offering one-year PGCEs, our course was structured to meet both the government requirements of circular 24/89 and the current CATE criteria. Our aim was to provide a high quality, coherent programme of training and support for potential primary teachers. The students have diverse backgrounds, knowledge (both in breadth and depth) and various skills and abilities. In short, each has different needs as far as the nature and quantity of support and preparation for teaching are concerned. Many of these needs were (and are) satisfied in the university. There are resources and facilities to do so, and staff and expertise. Student experience and opportunity on school placements inevitably varied, not only between schools but also within them.[1] Conflict could arise because the class teacher was unsure of her or his role in the training programme. Some students are adept at using such conflict to their own advantage. There was a tendency for some teachers to be critical of student practice without providing suggestions for how to improve. Students often expressed frustration at the nature of support and the lack of progression within schools and across schools, as they moved into subsequent school experiences.

The Diagnostic Monitoring Project, which began in Spring 1992 as a small-scale pilot project with only a few schools and students, was intended to address such matters. As a model it has run alongside more conventional forms of student supervision in which support and assessment were the responsibility of the university and involved frequent tutor visits. An increasing number of schools has become involved each year in the DMP, in which the responsibility for support and supervision has been largely given to the schools.

SUPPORTING STUDENT LEARNING

Practice and Diagnostic Monitoring: The Rationale

Study of various training programmes shows that three elements are important in developing new skills: knowledge, time and practice.[2] Practice is particularly important because it helps to integrate knowledge and to support its assimilation to the point where it can be deployed as coherent, orchestrated strategies, rather than as unconnected fragments, often hesitantly recalled and timidly applied.[3] It is known that certain kinds of support during practice facilitate this process of assimilation. In particular, consistent diagnostic monitoring is effective in bringing about development of expertise. This is the process of identifying strengths and weaknesses in student teachers' competences, and providing guidance for building on those strengths and eliminating weaknesses. It is intended to be a positive, supporting process which builds confidence and expertise.

The structure within which we perceive the student teacher's progress from novice to non-expert to newly-qualified teacher is shown in Figure 6.1. The novice teacher first gains an awareness of the teaching context through an initial school experience, then acquires knowledge of requirements, expectations, goals, subject matter and teaching strategies, with some simulated experience, role play exercises and observation of practising teachers. The novice then practises some basic skills and approaches in a school and deepens the process of development.

At the same time they are expected to supplement or enhance their knowledge during that experience. During this second school experience the student generally operates at the level of non-expert. A non-expert teacher tends to be more successful than the novice in that they are aware of a broader range of skills, knowledge and understanding accessible to them, and have had opportunities to think about and practise some of them. However, they are not yet expert in these competences and tend to orchestrate them in a somewhat forced and laboured way. (This point will be returned to later.)

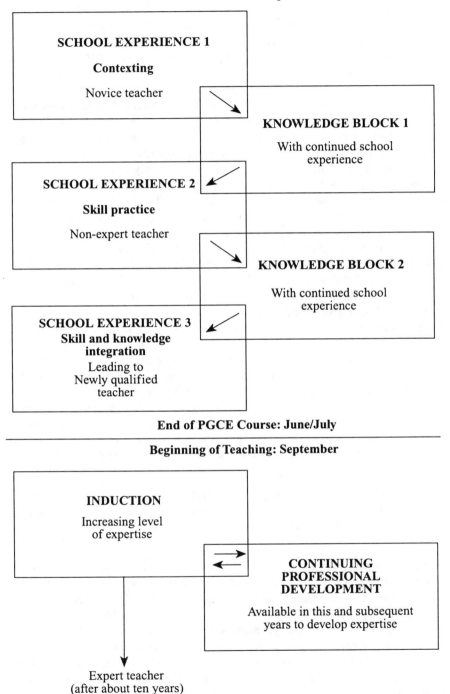

Figure 6.1 THE NATURE AND SEQUENCE OF EXPERIENCES

This non-expert teacher then acquires more knowledge and refines that already held, supported by directed tasks and focused observations of good practice in schools. This, in turn, is followed by a prolonged period of practice with the aim of increasing the level of expertise and knowledge to an acceptable level for newly qualified status.

Figure 6.1 shows the balance of development occurring in each context and at each stage of training. The overlapping blocks indicate that knowledge and skills are to be acquired in both contexts. The role of both supporting teacher and university tutor in this process is vital. Without structured support and guidance progress can be erratic, uneven and sometimes non-existent. As a consequence inappropriate practices and attitudes may develop.

The newly qualified teacher is far from being an expert teacher. Once newly qualified status is achieved there should be a period of induction during which support and continuing professional development are available to aid further progress. Achieving the level of expert teacher takes time. Chase and Simon (1973) studied expertise in chess. Drawing an analogy with chess, mental skills (like planning and management skills), knowledge and understanding of the opponent (how children respond, behave and learn), and what strategies and tactics are available (methods and approaches) are all brought to the game (teaching). Chase and Simon observed that to become an expert requires more than having innate natural abilities to play the game. The player must develop a repertoire of tactics that can be brought into play, given a particular board position. They suggest it takes about ten years of dedicated practice to become a grandmaster. This does not seem too far removed from what is needed to be an expert teacher. The university provides the novice and non-expert teacher with the rules of the game, how to start, develop and end a game, good moves to make in difficult positions, and the strategies and tactics for achieving particular ends. The schools provide the opportunities to use and practise these moves, following the rules. Garnham and Oakhill (1994) state that:

> There are many parallels between mental skills and other skills . . . to reach a high degree of proficiency can take a long time – mental skills, like manual skills, can take many years to develop.
>
> (p. 224)

A study of the differences in learning between novices and experts was carried out by Larkin (1979, 1983). Experts not only know more than novices, they also store and organise the information differently in their long-term memory. They encode new information more quickly and draw upon it more effectively to use for problem solving. Experts tend to 'chunk' the information, whereas novices work with single units and have naive and superficial representations of problems and situations (Priest and Lindsay, 1992). Such studies have implications for the development of student teachers' competences.

COMPETENCES AND DIAGNOSTIC MONITORING

For novices to progress to the non-expert level, they are expected to acquire a range of professional competences.[4] These include:

a Knowing the subjects they are expected to teach and understanding the National Curriculum requirements for those subjects.

b Being able to apply this knowledge and understanding in the planning for and delivery of relevant learning experiences suited to the needs and abilities of the learners.

c Understanding how pupils learn in order to plan, monitor progress, assess and record that progress.

d Being familiar with national standards and procedures for summative assessment.

e Acquiring a range of teaching skills and strategies important for class management, organisation and control, and using them appropriately.

These competences are not discrete units, rather each is a piece of the jigsaw in the development of a confident and competent newly qualified teacher. Similarly, the acquisition of competences is not the totality of initial teacher training. The process is informed by our own and other research into teaching and learning, for the aim is not simply to produce skilled craftsmen by apprenticeship. Rather, it is to produce teachers who possess their own 'practical theory of teaching' which guides their educational practice (Handal and Lauvas, 1993) and also develop in them the ability to reflect on that theory and practice, that is, become reflective teachers (Schon, 1983; Mackinnon, 1993).

Diagnostic monitoring can relate to the quality of the performance in any or all of these competences and will need to take into account the stage of training. Some kind of observation schedule is, therefore, useful for monitoring the acquisition and practice of such competences.

During the second school experience it might be expected that teaching competences would be evident at a lower level than in the final, long school experience. The difference may be less one of quantity than of quality and efficiency in deployment and of integrated deployment of strategies. Skills may be practised in relative isolation, and without fine-tuning and precision. In the earlier stage it must be remembered that students will not have had the opportunity to acquire all the knowledge and understanding expected. Some will come from school experience two and knowledge block one. They should also acquire more during school experience two and knowledge block two. During school experience three there is the opportunity to improve the quality, assimilation and integration of skills, so evidence of development in that direction is expected. The process of reaching full expertise needs time, and this does not usually occur until after the period of induction and continuing professional development.

In school experiences two and three diagnostic monitoring is intended to identify where progress is being made and where support is needed. It informs the process of guiding the student towards greater expertise. As well as structuring and supporting that process the evaluation schedule provides a uniform means of reporting on progress, which will be familiar to students in whatever school they practise. This familiarity also allows them to carry out self-assessment and shape their own development.

FINAL ASSESSMENT OF PROGRESS

Towards the end of the final school experience it is necessary to assess attainment and provide evidence of competence for newly qualified teacher status. Any NQT must have demonstrated that they have:

a   Sufficient knowledge of the subjects of the National Curriculum to enable them to meet most of the requirements for the relevant Key Stage.
b   Sufficient understanding of how pupils learn in order to plan learning experiences appropriate to needs and abilities.
c   Sufficient understanding in the process of assessment to assess learning and behavioural outcomes.
d   Sufficient organisational, management and control skills to provide a classroom environment conducive to learning.
e   Appropriate professional attitudes and behaviours.

Evidence which indicates an acceptable level of expertise or competence would be that in most instances the student is planning lessons and activities with:

a   Accurate subject content.
b   Content matched to the needs and abilities of the pupils.
c   A range of strategies, approaches and resources.

They should also show that they are:

d   Monitoring and assessing children's progress appropriately and acting on the evidence in future planning.
e   Managing, organising and controlling the class in a way which provides a safe environment which supports and encourages learning.
f   Relating well to pupils, teachers and other significant adults most of the time.

Inadequate levels of expertise would be reflected in the quality of the pupils' learning and/or the student's professional relationships, attitudes and behaviours. Each situation tends to be unique but generalisations are possible to develop guidelines; for example, if the class teacher had to re-teach most of the work. Instances of such behaviour might be an inability to control the class to a level which allows learning to take place with the majority of pupils most of the time; or an inability to relate to and work with the class as a whole, although perhaps being able to work with individuals and small groups of pupils quite well; or an inability to match the level of work or activities to the needs and abilities of the pupils. However, such occurrences should be relatively rare, given the purpose of diagnostic monitoring and the role of the supporting teacher.

THE ROLE OF THE SUPPORTING TEACHER

In partnership the supporting teacher is seen as having a role which goes beyond that which was customary. The task of writing a job description for such a teacher is difficult. The role is as diverse and varied as teaching itself. However, in essence it is seen as one of encouraging the novice teacher to be more aware of her or his perceptions of primary teaching and learning through a process of discussion, reflection and critical evaluation. This requires a shift in quality and quantity of structured support given to the novice by the supporting teacher. Some basic guidance for such communication includes:

* observe with sensitivity to needs and effort made;
* use jargon-free language, agreed and recognised by all in the training process;
* observe with a focus in mind, negotiated with and understood by the novice teacher;
* advise rather than judge, emphasising what is positive;
* offer possible strategies or solutions as ways forward in dealing with the problems or difficulties;
* value what is done according to the stage of training and the needs of the individual;
* share observations, ideas and experiences so as to work with the student teacher in the learning process.

The nature of the support which the novice primary teachers need will obviously change as they progress from novice to non-expert to newly-qualified teachers. The development of their professional competence and confidence is not a linear or uniform process. It is complex and involves a shift in focus from self (the student teacher) to others (the pupil learners). Maynard and Furlong (1992) recognised five distinct stages in this development:

1 Early idealism. The student teacher's approach to teaching and learning is influenced by her or his own school experiences as a pupil and emulation plays a significant role.
2 Survival. The student teacher's ability to organise, manage and control the teaching and learning environment become the focus, with rejection of some models and approaches because of risks involved.

3   Recognition of difficulties. Once the student teacher feels she or he has some mastery of management and control of the class as a whole, the focus shifts to the individuals within it, and the quality of interaction, match and motivation.
4   Complacency plateau. At this stage the student teacher is self-satisfied and feels that her or his performance is acceptable to both supporting teacher and tutor and becomes complacent.
5   Moving forward. Through evaluation and reflection the student teacher's needs now become ones of ensuring the best quality of experiences being offered to pupils.

It is interesting to note that HMI, in their inspections of secondary school-based partnership models, have found that teacher-mentors are having difficulty supporting students in going beyond the complacency plateau (Baker, 1994). She described how developmental messages were lost as students reached their 'performance ceiling' and the mentors were not forceful enough in pushing them beyond this point.

THE ROLE OF THE UNIVERSITY TUTOR

O'Hara (1994) suggests primary schools have no tradition or expertise in the training of new teachers, nor are they designed or structured for this function. The results of numerous recent surveys would suggest they have no real desire to do so (for example, the Standing Conference of Principals 1994). Such results indicate that the HEIs have a very clear role to play in partnership, by providing:

- course stability;
- programme overview;
- structure and coherence to programmes;
- moderation across experiences;
- contexts for reflection and analysis;
- breadth of resources and expertise;
- curriculum expertise;
- pedagogical foundations for practice.

This role clearly complements that of the supporting teacher.

DIAGNOSTIC MONITORING PROJECT STAGE ONE

Both as course director and as a supervising tutor I wanted to tap into and build upon the excellent work which was being done by some teachers. I decided to begin with my own tutor group on the eight-week school placement in the summer term of 1992. Seven teachers and their students in five schools in the Newcastle area were willing to help. I was able to offer these schools £100 per student as a token of appreciation for the extra work which the project produced. My initial aims were quite modest: to improve the quality of communication between the class teachers, the students and myself to ensure that we all had common perceptions of needs and expectations. I felt there should be some common agreement on how we support our students and our expectations of them.

Prior to the teaching practice, during the students' preliminary observation days, I visited the schools and discussed the project with the headteachers and classteachers concerned. Both were given copies of a very brief outline of the purpose and aims of the project and how these aims could be achieved. The outline also contained a copy of a draft lesson/activity evaluation schedule and offered a list of criteria on which to judge students' work. There was also a summative assessment form, linked to these criteria. The classteachers would support the students as they usually did. In addition, they would take on a more supervisory and evaluative role by doing the following:

- Observing at least one complete lesson/set of activities each week, according to the criteria, and completing an evaluation schedule.
- Using the evaluation for discussion and debriefing with the student after the session observed, and setting targets for the next week.
- Considering the appropriateness of the evaluation schedule for the task.
- Varying the content-focus of the sessions observed over the school experience so as to cover as much of the curriculum as possible.
- Keeping notes on perceptions of and feelings about working this way and the increased responsibility involved, to be passed to me at the end of the practice.
- Completing a summative report form and, again, considering its suitability for purpose.

Before the practice began I went through the project in detail with my students, dealing with their queries and making sure they were happy to be involved. Their response was very positive.

Evaluation of Stage One

There was an evaluation meeting after the practice ended. The aim was to see if the teachers and students felt that the project was of any value and, if so, how it should develop. The meeting was structured with a set of questions which focused attention on key issues. These will be discussed in turn.

1 Did You Enjoy Working in this Way?

All the teachers enjoyed it. Three qualified this with comments reflecting upon the quality of the students, for example:

> Yes, because she was a good student . . . I might not have felt the same if she had been a poor student.

2 How Did You Feel about the Idea of Handing over More Responsibility to You in this Way?

All felt that as a way of working it had been successful and were happy to continue, but again commented that this was probably due to the quality of the student, for example:

> It hasn't been as bad as I thought because the student's okay. It would have been more difficult if she had been failing.

> There could have been conflict if she hadn't been a good student or if there had been a personality clash.

One teacher was very positive, seeing the model as having the advantage of focusing his mind on the student, and also acknowledging his professionalism since he felt he was the person who knew the class best and was best placed to monitor the student's progress. He also felt that he could offer more immediate and relevant advice. This same teacher saw the key to the success of such a model as being the quality of the school and teacher used – these, he felt, were crucial to the scheme.

3 Were There any Problems with Adopting a Dual Role of Teacher/Supporter and Tutor/Assessor?

Half of the teachers felt there had been no problems. One teacher said:

> There was no conflict. The only way out of criticism is to be positive and work together. The early stages of working together are essential to give warning signs.

The other teachers did express some initial discomfort:

> It is difficult to be two roles – supporter and critical evaluator.

> Conflict or alienation becomes a source of problems.

> Saying things positively and still being supportive – I'm not trained for this.

The importance of the tutor was emphasised in this context.

4 Would Some Kind of Prior Training Have Helped?

All of the teachers answered positively to this. Several areas were suggested into which could be built some preparation for the role. These were:

- Knowing the broader programme which the students had experienced.
- Considering the variety of ways of working with and supporting students.
- Having more time to think about and discuss what is expected and what to look for.

- Considering the terms and interpretation of the criteria.
- Considering the levels of performance of students at different stages of training.
- Having practice runs with the evaluation schedules.

In addition details of the students' earlier experiences and performance and of their levels of competence and needs were suggested.

5 What Is the Role of the Headteacher?

All the teachers felt the head's role was overseeing the total experience, and being available for consultation and advice. The head was also seen in the role of training and supporting the classteachers to work with students.

6 What Is the Role of the University Tutor?

The tutor was seen as a vital link between student, teacher, school and university. Most of the teachers felt that the tutor would be as much a support to the teachers as to the students. Since students are so variable the success of such a scheme was seen as depending very much on the quality and type of student. If the teacher was thoroughly prepared and the student was not particularly problematic, the tutor's role might be limited. However, the weaker the student, the more teamwork would be needed between the classteacher and tutor. In addition, where personality clashes occurred, the tutor would need to mediate. Moderation and assessment of practice across teachers and schools was also seen as important, as was the actual selection of schools and teachers for the task. One teacher pointed out:

> It's not just getting the right school, it's getting the right teacher. You might get a good class teacher but he or she cannot impart their expertise to students.

There were strong feelings that the tutors could not simply put students into schools and then 'abandon them' to their fate with the teacher. It had to be a joint enterprise.

7 What about the Timing – Other Practices?

Doing this for the autumn term school experience was seen by all teachers as being more problematic, because they were still establishing their own relationships with the new class.

8 What Did You Feel about the Evaluation Schedule?

Completing the forms once a week was seen as 'about right', with more frequency if appropriate. The list of criteria (skills and competences) was seen as a useful cue sheet for focusing observations. The evaluation sheet itself worked well on lessons with a single subject focus but the infant teachers operating integrated activities found it less useful. The criteria had been clustered (e.g. planning, discipline and control, interaction skills) with a small box adjacent to each cluster in which to write. The boxes were seen as too limiting and led to repetition at times. They suggested a reorganisation with larger, more open comment boxes, which the other teachers considered equally acceptable. Once they had got used to how to use it, all the teachers felt the 'ways forward' box was the most important part of the sheet, as it really focused thinking on the student's needs. However, this aspect had been initially difficult to deal with and needed more emphasis during the preparation stage.

9 What Did You Feel about the Summative Report Form?

All were happy with the structure of the form. Once again, as with the evaluation schedule, it focused on clusters of skills and competences, requiring a summative statement about each cluster. The teachers used evidence from the evaluation sheets to complete these statements. The timing of the report form's completion was more problematic, as was the quality of pass (shades of grey between pass and fail). The issue of failing students (none in the pilot group) was discussed in this context, and the importance of early warning of this and independent assessment by the university tutor was discussed. It was also suggested that in addition to discussing the report form with the students, there might be a space for the students to complete for themselves.

10 Have You any Other Points?

The general response was that, for most of them, once they had got used to it they had enjoyed working this way. One teacher said:

I enjoyed it. It wasn't much more than I would do anyway.

However, concerns were expressed about the pressures and stresses on primary teachers in times of change. Under heavy pressure already, the change of role would not be welcomed by many. Inevitably, staffing problems and money were mentioned. A further point was that it was better for students and teachers where there were at least two students in the school. This gave both students and teachers opportunities to share perceptions and talk together about the process.

The Students' Perspective

From the students' viewpoint what came through clearly was that they all thought they had had a much more structured and supportive experience than previously. They felt that classteachers had clearer expectations and the quality of communication and interaction was good. The students also felt that knowing that I was still around in the background was reassuring. They valued the time out with me to share feelings with someone from outside the school. They suggested that they be given copies of the evaluation schedules to do some self- and paired-evaluations to help them in the process of reflecting on practice.

DIAGNOSTIC MONITORING PROJECT STAGE TWO

Having found from this pilot study that this way of working was feasible and could produce desirable outcomes, I extended it in the following summer term (1993). An interested colleague also agreed to be involved with her tutor group. The evaluations from the previous year had indicated that some prior training was needed. A preparation day out of school, with supply cover paid for, was organised.

A review of research into supporting student teachers in training and practice was used to produce a longer, more detailed booklet for the project. The evaluation schedule and summative report form were also amended in line with the teachers' comments.

We approached all headteachers in the schools with which my colleague and I would be working, outlined what was involved to the headteacher and asked them for time to discuss it with their staff. Involvement was entirely voluntary so we were pleased to find that nearly all the schools agreed to participate. This gave us twenty-one teachers in thirteen schools, which meant approximately one-quarter of the cohort of students would be involved in the DMP.

As before we went through everything in detail with the students beforehand. We also gave them copies of the evaluation schedule to use for self-evaluation purposes and a copy of the report form for them to complete at the end of the placement. They were asked to keep notes on how they felt the project worked for them so that we could evaluate it once again at the end of the year.

The preparation day was held before the Easter break but after the students had begun to make their serial visits to the schools for the final practice. In it we attempted to cover the points raised in the pilot study. Using video material of students in classrooms, use of the evaluation schedule was given. We also asked one of the teachers from the pilot study to talk with the group about his experience.

An additional and unexpected aspect was that HMI would be visiting schools as part of the inspection of the primary PGCE course. The reporting HMI was told of the project and he felt it appropriate to visit some of the DMP schools as well as those where students were being supervised in a more conventional way.

Evaluation of Stage Two

At the end of the practice we invited the teachers and students to attend an evaluation meeting in the university. Once again we tried to focus the discussion on key questions, but because the group was much larger it was more difficult to do so. Generally, many of the comments echoed those of the previous year:

• An initial apprehension over the change in role and increase in responsibility involved.

- The importance of both the quality of the student and the ability of the teacher to work with and support students.
- The need to know more about the students' previous experiences and performances.
- The revised evaluation schedule was, generally, liked and served as a very useful *aide mémoire* for observing and discussing practice.
- The summative report form caused some confusion as to who filled in the 'pass/fail' box on the front cover, although the teachers seemed happier with the elimination of shades of pass or fail, and suggested that the box could be larger so that a qualifying statement could be added should the school wish to do so (for example, to emphasise a very good student's performance which would have been recorded simply as a pass).

By this stage the government's plans for school-based training partnerships were known and, as far as secondary training was concerned, models were already being discussed and put in place. Anticipation of the implications of such a directive for primary training inevitably coloured some of the discussion during the evaluation session with a degree of nervousness. It would appear that for the teachers in the associate schools working with the DMP model, it was this far and no further, a point I will return to later.

DIAGNOSTIC MONITORING PROJECT: STAGE THREE

By this stage (1994) Circular 14/93 on primary training had been received and working groups established to consider how we were to move into partnership with schools. It was decided to extend the DMP to involve all primary tutors (though not all students and schools). This was to give all tutors experience in the project. Internal funding was made available by the head of department, which would allow the involvement of more students and their classteachers. All schools which had previously been involved were included, plus a selection to cover other tutor groups. Tutors approached headteachers first and, once again, the response was positive. The final number of participants was eleven tutors and thirty-five students and their classteachers in twenty-four schools. This represented over one-third of the student cohort.

As before, a preparation day was organised, taking into account comments made at the evaluation session. In addition, we focused on:

- improving the quality of the documentation;
- developing agreed terminology;
- identifying roles of the participants more clearly.

This was done by combining what we had learned from the experiences so far with evidence from research and what was happening elsewhere. Figure 6.2 is a copy of the programme for that day. As with the previous year an evaluation session at the end of the practice suggested general satisfaction with this way of working. The DMP was proving to be an acceptable level of responsibility for teachers, so long as they were supported by university tutors in this role *and* there was financial support to the schools. Teachers, students and tutors were, generally, happy with the evaluation schedule. The report form also generated no adverse comment. The focus was very much on providing more and better information to teachers about students' prior experiences and levels of competence so that the supporting teachers could build upon this. With this in mind a target for the following year to develop profiles and action plans was set.

IN CONCLUSION

How should the partnership between our associate schools and the university develop in order to meet the requirements of Circular 14/93? During the full HMI inspection of the primary PGCE at Newcastle which took place in May and October 1993, the team of inspectors visited eighteen primary (or equivalent) schools during the students' final school placement in one week in May. Of the thirty-four students seen, half were in schools involved in the DMP. The remainder were involved in conventional supervision placements. The HMI were briefed on the project and its aims and given the documentation used. They were therefore able to comment on its suitability as a model for development of partnership.

In the summary of the main findings, the report states:

> Some schools were assuming an enhanced role in the assessment of students . . . [which] . . . worked well in some cases, but was still at an early stage at the time of the inspection . . . teachers who had undergone training for the project were developing valuable skills in the assessment of competences.

> (HMI, 1994, para. 71)

Using the experiences from the DMP, a more prominent role for schools is envisaged, with teachers being particularly well placed to help students develop classroom skills. However, an increase in the time spent in schools and greater attention preparing for the core subjects of the National Curriculum all have their costs. Given that any involvement in the training of teachers is optional for schools, the commitment to the new training role is therefore voluntary for the primary schools. The key question is, will the 170 or so schools with which we have existing working relationships volunteer for this greater involvement which, of necessity, means more responsibility, more time and more work? If O'Hara's (1994) findings are anything to go by this is unlikely. Therefore, at Newcastle we have decided to move more cautiously. Although we have the DMP model in place with about one-third of associate schools we decided

PRIMARY POSTGRADUATE CERTIFICATE IN EDUCATION

SUPPORTING STUDENT LEARNING

PRACTICE AND DIAGNOSTIC

MONITORING PROJECT

PREPARATION DAY

Friday 11 February 1994
9.15 a.m. to 3.15 p.m.
ROOM G.20
SCHOOL OF EDUCATION

Programme

9.00 a.m.   Arrival, Registration and Coffee

9.15 a.m.   **Introduction:** The Context
                   - Outline of the Primary PGCE course, Aims of the Project.

                   Diagnostic Monitoring:
                   - What is it? Outline and use of the Standard Evaluation Schedule

                   Using the Schedule:
                   - VIDEO 1: preliminary views of monitoring and assessment,
                   - Discussion

10.30 a.m.   Coffee Break

10.50 a.m.   **Supporting students teaching the core subjects**
                   - English, Mathematics and Science
                   - VIDEO 2: assessing general practice

12.00 noon   Lunch

12.45 p.m.   **Supporting students teaching other subjects**
                   - e.g. Technology, P.E., Art.

                   Advising and Reporting
                   - importance of discussion and feedback
                   - VIDEO 3: Discussion

2.15 p.m.   Tea

2.35 p.m.   **A teacher's view:**
                   - supporting students using diagnostic monitoring
                   - Final questions and discussion

Figure 6.2

not to push for a full partnership model for September 1994. Rather, we aim to build a model for partnership which could accommodate the diversity of opinion on the nature of teacher training in the primary school.

Immediately following the release of Circular 14/93 a small group of six headteachers, all volunteers representing the interests of the five LEAs with which we work most frequently, formed an initial working group to discuss the situation with the five core primary tutors. From this meeting, we planned a programme for development over the next twelve months. The first stage was to survey all of the headteachers of the 170 associate schools to determine their views on partnership. Of the 102 (60 per cent) respondents, there seemed a genuine desire on the part of most for a much closer working relationship in the training process, going beyond mere tokenism. However, like the results of national surveys, headteachers expressed no real interest in taking sole responsibility for the training of new teachers and saw the university's involvement as crucial. Versions of the DMP seem likely to provide ways of working with which many will be happy. From the headteachers' comments, it will, however, take goodwill, patience and the three Cs: co-operation, communication and co-ordination.

NOTES

1. It is interesting to note that this problem has not been resolved under the new partnership arrangements for secondary courses. Tysome (1994) reports on the failure of the scheme in some areas because the schools are not doing what is expected of them and, indeed, what they are being paid to do, and not using the money for mentor release to train and support student teachers.

2. Garnham and Oakhill (1994) provide a useful review of the importance of the balance between knowledge, time and practice, covering the research from the last twenty years on novices and experts working in various professional and other fields.

3. See, for instance, the work of Yekovich *et al.* (1991), interpreting the studies of Anzai and Simon (1979) and other theories of learning by doing.

4. Taken from the CATE (1993) list of competences, published with Circular 14/93. This is an amended version of the list we used when the Diagnostic Monitoring Project first began.

5. For example the SCOP survey, the results of which were published in January 1994.

MENTORING: AN EXAMINATION OF SOME KEY ISSUES IN TWO SCHOOLS

Wayne Jones

INTRODUCTION

The increasingly prominent role which schools are playing in the arena of Initial Teacher Training is being given a cautious welcome by many involved in education as a way of fostering partnerships between schools and training institutions. At the same time, however, one might suspect that the government has a hidden agenda which aims to curtail the influences of radical training institutions and/or seeks a means of training teachers 'on the cheap'. Government rhetoric typically acknowledges problems but assures us all that its intentions are good:

> Too often in the past, schools involved in teacher training have been left unclear about their role . . . Schools have lacked the resources and teachers have lacked the time to carry out their training tasks effectively. Both have often felt poor relations alongside the training institutions. For the future, I want to ensure that schools and experienced teachers involved in training students know what they are supposed to be doing and have the training, the time and the resources to be able to it well.
> (Clarke, 1992, pp. 5–6)

Welcome reassurances, but how much has been offered so far to fulfil such promises? A change in the structure of teacher training courses which is not accompanied by a mechanism which prepares teachers for their new role will achieve little. The teachers' perception of this new role is one of the foundations upon which school-based training rests. If mentoring is perceived as 'having a student', and a means of getting more free time, and if trainees are 'thrown in at the deep end' or at best learn through 'sitting with Nellie' then the partnership has little value. Furthermore, it is important that mentoring is recognised as being more complex than merely pointing out the gap between a trainee's capabilities and those of an ideal teacher.

One of the aims of this chapter is to examine how mentors perceive their changing role in teacher training and the extent to which they feel equipped to perform their function effectively.

Developments in initial teacher training have largely been initiated either by training institutions or the government and its agencies. The schools have generally been the passive recipients of schemes or courses invented elsewhere. Although schools are now being given more control and influence in the training of teachers, they rarely give this area of their activities a high priority. How often, for example, does it appear as a central feature on a school's management plan? If schools are to adapt to change can these issues remain on the margins of their agenda?

'The rhetoric of partnership is easy; the reality of partnership is much more difficult to achieve.' (Burrell and Sexton, in Alexander, 1980, p. 108). It is one of the aims of this chapter to attempt to explore this reality; to provide an opportunity for those involved in teacher training in one primary and one secondary school engaged in the University of Sussex PGCE partnership to explore issues, concerns and needs.

George IV Comprehensive is an 11–18 mixed school in East Sussex with approximately 1,300 pupils. The school was invited to join the University of Sussex partnership scheme in 1991. The professional tutor is a senior teacher who has carried overall responsibility for trainees for several years.

De Montfort Primary School is a 3–11 school with 390 pupils serving a varied catchment in Lewes, East Sussex. It has been involved with the Partnership Scheme for several years, usually taking two or three trainees. The professional tutor is the headteacher. Three members of staff are mentors.

Interviews were carried out with all the mentors in both schools, the professional tutor at George IV and one teacher at George IV whose classes had been taken by a trainee. In order to avoid interviewing trainees who were currently engaged in the course and who therefore might be guarded in their responses, a group of six George IV teachers who completed their training at Sussex were selected. Two of these had not been placed at George IV in their PGCE year and they were therefore able to provide some insight into mentoring activities in other schools. Four of these interviewees are women, two of whom had been mature students when they undertook their PGCE.

The chapter opens with the responses of interviewees regarding the position of the mentor within the school structure, and the extent to which they feel equipped for their role. This is followed by an examination of the training and skills which mentors feel that they need. Issues relating to monitoring the work of mentors and the consistency of experience offered to trainees are then explored. Aspects of the particular dynamic of the mentor/trainee relationship are touched upon before the section closes with the benefits which mentors perceive as arising from their role.

THE MENTOR'S ROLE

Dart and Drake (1993) found that the mentors involved in the Sussex partnership scheme include males and females of differing ages, professional experience and status within their departments. At George IV and De Montfort, however, this is not the case; in these schools all the mentors have positions of responsibility and/or are very experienced teachers. At George IV heads of department decide who will be the mentor for their subject, but at De Montfort the opportunity is open to any member of staff. At George IV three mentors are co-ordinators of faculty, two are heads of department and one is a second in faculty. At De Montfort one is deputy head, one is head of the junior department and the third is an experienced teacher with responsibility for special needs. Responsibility for newly qualified teachers at George IV, however, almost always lies with the second in department. The professional tutor at George IV explains:

> We have a great responsibility in training students and the mentor should really be an experienced teacher. The NQTs have had their training and only need support, which can be provided by someone other than a head of department.

As Dart and Drake observe, heads of department are likely to have had experience of more than one school, they have more non-contact time and their seniority gives them control over the trainee's timetable. Dart and Drake also note that some schools see mentoring as a professional development opportunity for younger members of the department. Although no conscious decision has been made at either George IV or De Montfort to restrict the opportunity to experienced teachers, it is interesting that in all cases the head of department or, at De Montfort, senior teachers, have taken the responsibility themselves.

When asked why they had decided to become mentors many of the interviewees declared that they considered it a challenge. A few admitted that they had hoped it would create some time for them, an expectation that, with hindsight, they recognised as naive!

One of the trainees interviewed insisted that the mentors should not be heads of department because they are 'busy people who cannot really devote sufficient of their precious time to mentoring'. Although her mentor had generally made herself available the trainee always felt that she was imposing on her mentor's time. All the mentors interviewed stressed that although their mentoring activities had created great demands on their time, they had prioritised their mentoring at the expense of other aspects of their responsibility because they enjoyed it or felt they had a duty to the trainee. The perception remains on the part of this trainee, however, that she was a nuisance. The hour per week currently funded for mentoring time is therefore vital because both mentor and trainee recognise this as their time which does not encroach on other activities.

It would seem crucial that this tutorial time is preserved, inadequate as it is, as a means of not only providing space for mentor and trainee to talk, but as a way of preventing trainees from feeling that they are imposing on their mentors.

A mentor at George IV observed that if the scheme is operated by high status figures in the school it will be seen to have high status, which he feels is important to raise the profile of mentoring within the school. There is, however, a price to pay for this. The same mentor pointed out that schools are being reimbursed for providing mentoring time at the cheapest rate but at George IV the time of the mentors, being heads of department, is more costly and so the school suffers financially.

Trainees in secondary schools, unlike primary schools, are usually attached to more than one member of a department. At George IV trainees take the classes of three or four teachers within each department, although contact with other members of staff obviously contributes to their learning. The advantages of this range of contact, according to mentors and trainees interviewed, are that a variety of teaching styles are observed, several sources of advice exist and other staff can gain the experience which comes from working with trainees. There would appear to be some disadvantages, however: one mentor felt that he is not sufficiently aware of the techniques being employed by other staff when observing, feeding back and assessing. Another mentor added:

> The other staff do not record in enough detail the kind of information I need to assess the trainee, whereas if the trainee is taking your own class you obviously have an idea of the things which aren't necessarily recorded on paper.

One teacher interviewed, who is not a mentor but has a heavy involvement with the trainee, felt very strongly that because of time pressures:

> I have to speak to her during snatched moments in the staffroom, in the car commuting between sites and over the lunch table. With a good student, we can just about get by, but with a weak student this would be catastrophic.

There would appear to be two issues here:

- creating time for members of staff other than mentors to meet with trainees is something which schools would find very difficult to achieve;
- there is a need for intra-school communication and training regarding observation, feedback and assessment so that all staff are equipped to work with trainees.

The trainees interviewed generally welcomed the breadth of advice which being involved with a number of teachers had provided. When conflicting advice was given they felt, in general, able to evaluate it, although one trainee described a situation where this was not so easy:

> My mentor was quite progressive regarding his attitude to the teaching

of basics and he was dead against teaching spelling rules. The teacher of my Year 7 class wanted me to deliver a programme of spelling. When I asked my mentor what strategies I could use to teach the rules he told me that it was a waste of time bothering. I ended up by teaching spelling in secret!

Those involved in teacher training acknowledge the dynamic that is often set up between training institution and school where a trainee has to satisfy the demands of both and where there can be, on occasion, a conflict of advice. Not enough recognition has been given, however, to the tension set up when a trainee receives conflicting advice within the same institution.

Another issue raised here is that in primary schools the range of staff with whom a trainee comes into contact is small; they are often attached to the class of one teacher. The De Montfort mentors recognised that the trainees are therefore restricted to a single role model unless opportunities are created for observing other teachers.

TRAINING AND SKILLS

There is a significant difference between trainees and mentors in what they view as the skills which a mentor should possess. Perhaps predictably all the trainees interviewed considered those skills to be important which foster the trainee's growth, 'a developed sense of development' as one put it. Others stressed the ability to encourage, 'especially as everyone feels demoralised most of the time'. They should be able to listen, give support, be fair, open-minded and diplomatic. One interviewee felt that a mentor should be 'less professional, less formal and more approachable'. She also suggested that mentors should 'possess an ability to seem interested'!

Although the mentors' comments echo some of the above, they considered the skills of mentoring to be more wide-ranging. Some mentors placed an emphasis not so much on skills relating to trainee development as on those necessary to preserve the mentor's own survival:

To be able to juggle another egg.
To cope with being watched and trailed.
To manage time effectively.
To have the strength to say: 'I haven't time to discuss it now'.

Or the survival of the mentor's classes:

To resist leaping in to rescue the lesson.
To avoid bawling kids out when you are supposed to be observing.
To be able to relinquish your favourite group to somebody else.

At a training day for new mentors held at the university, areas of concern were brainstormed. It is interesting that nowhere on the list of twenty-two items that was drawn up was there a desire for training in the skills necessary for fostering the trainees' development through self-evaluation, observation and giving feedback. Yet most of the experienced mentors interviewed for this study felt that these activities figured among *their* training needs. This suggests that an awareness of a need for such skills only arises after one has had some experience of mentoring.

Other training needs voiced by mentors included being given a greater awareness of what mentoring activities consist of. The primary mentors especially felt that they needed to know more about the aims of the course. Although all mentors were aware that the material supplied by the university covers some of this, most only referred to it when completing reports.

Just as there is a significance in the new mentors' lack of awareness of certain training needs, a similar omission from the experienced mentors' lists is interesting. Lacey (1977) traces the various stages that PGCE trainees may pass through on their course: 'honeymoon', 'the search for material and ways of teaching', 'the crisis', etc. Some mentors interviewed for this study displayed an implicit awareness of stages in the development of the trainees with whom they had worked, but none seemed to recognise that such stages could occur generally in the trainees' experience. It could be argued that an explicit awareness of such aspects of teacher training would be of benefit to both the mentor and the trainee.

Many mentors foster trainee self-evaluation through the use of self-evaluation sheets and by asking trainees to evaluate lesson plans:

> It is important to try to get trainees to step away from the situation they are in – they can spend time coping with specifics. We need to get them to reflect on what they have done, not just on what they intend to do.

Mentors are aware that in self-evaluation trainees can be over-critical of their performance, but few think that they themselves have sufficient skills to be fully effective in ensuring that trainees reflect meaningfully on what they do.

MONITORING NEEDS

One need which emerged strongly through the discussions with mentors was their desire for feedback:

> I would like to feel confident and reassured that what I am doing is the right thing . . . I would like the opportunity of evaluating my observation skills . . . At our mentor meetings we are told in general that mentors are doing well, and we know that bad schools are 'removed' from the

> scheme, but we get nothing specific. I'd like to know that my judgements are consistent.

> I'd just like to know how I'm doing. After all, the kids expect to know, the students want to know, so why shouldn't we?

It is inevitable and perhaps, to a certain extent, desirable that every mentor will display individual approaches and attitudes to his or her work with trainees. The mentors at George IV and De Montfort between them offer quite a range:

> I see my job as getting them ready to 'go solo' . . . They watch me until they get it right and then I leave them with the classes. After that I keep the report criteria in front of me and tick things off as the student shows they can do it.

Unless feedback is provided, individuals such as the mentor quoted above will not realise that there are alternative approaches to the ones which they have adopted, such as development through self-evaluation and negotiated observation.

This need to provide feedback for mentors was also voiced by trainees. A trainee, who had been placed at a different school from the two case study school in the county, felt that his mentor had failed to perform his role effectively. Not only had there been no weekly meetings between mentor and trainee, but the trainee had hardly been observed. His reports had been almost entirely based on his self-evaluation. 'There was no one to tell the mentor where he was going wrong in strong enough terms . . . the mentor was out of my control.'

Another trainee felt that the university should monitor the mentor's assessments of trainees more carefully. In her view some trainees who didn't deserve qualified status were being passed by the schools. She saw this as sometimes resulting from the failure by the mentor to observe the trainee sufficiently to make judgements. One of her comments was particularly disturbing: 'After all, if the school passes a weak student it's not their problem any more and it rocks the boat far less than having to justify why a student has to be placed "At Risk".'

This comment highlights the problems inherent in considering the form which valuable feedback might take. It echoes the views which led Menter to conclude his study by stating:

> It has been demonstrated that stability is the dominant and overwhelming concern of all three parties [trainee, school and training institution]. School experience triads typically exhibit a property of stasis. All members of the triad seek to minimise, counteract or negate any influence or innovation which might upset the stability of the triad.
>
> (Menter, 1989)

To give schools the kind of feedback which would overcome the problems voiced above by trainees might risk upsetting the 'stability of the triad'. Although the needs of a trainee are a priority these have to be balanced against the survival of the partnership, especially when there is a finite number of schools in which to place a growing number of trainees and criticism of a school might fracture its relationship with the university.

The mentors recognised that to establish a mechanism which would provide the feedback which they so keenly require would not be a straightforward task. One asked: 'Are tutors going to come round and judge us?' Another felt that although the trainees would have opinions in this area, they were in no position to criticise the person who would be writing their reports until it would be too late to have any effect.

It would seem necessary to have some performance indicators against which one can judge mentors' achievements. It should be possible for the schools and university to establish a framework through which mentors can judge their own performance. The appraisal system has now been established in all schools. At the core of appraisal is self-evaluation and many teachers will therefore have had some experience of reflecting on their own performance. Furthermore, teachers are increasingly developing the pupils' ability to assess themselves and are therefore familiar with the strategies necessary to achieve this. It is also appropriate that the Sussex PGCE course, which seeks to develop its trainees as 'reflective practitioners', should foster mentor self-evaluation.

CONSISTENCY OF EXPERIENCE

Problems relating to having two trainees attached to one department were highlighted by interviewees. One trainee is not in favour of the idea:

> It is inevitable that one student will be better than another and in the eyes of the mentor this difference can appear to widen, to the benefit of the stronger student and the detriment of the weaker. Both students are aware that they are being compared and the weaker one's confidence suffers.

These apparent inconsistencies between the ways trainees are treated within one school can be seen within the framework of a wider issue: that of inconsistencies regarding the experiences trainees are offered between different schools. Many mentors and trainees interviewed voiced concerns over differences in the quality of experiences offered, and mentors were anxious that they were providing adequate support and breadth of training. The trainees were very aware that some schools were not apparently as supportive as others: 'It's difficult to do anything about it – it's built in to the system – but the implications for consistency of assessment are serious.'

CATE recognises this problem: 'HEI and all schools in partnership with them will need to collaborate in ensuring that students undertake similar

tasks and gain similar experience, wherever their time in school is spent.'
(1992, 3.1)

The new criteria attempt to address inconsistencies in the assessment of trainees and although a consideration of the effectiveness of these measures lies outside the scope of this chapter it is unlikely, in practice, that they will entirely remedy inequalities in the experiences offered to trainees by schools.

THE MENTOR AND THE TRAINEE

Students do funny things . . . they practically bring sandwiches for their mentor.

(Former Sussex trainee, now an NQT)

Menter notes that the shift from an apprenticeship approach in initial teacher training, whereby the trainee models the craft of an experienced teacher, towards an experiential approach where the trainee learns through doing, with the advice of experts, must change the nature of the role of mentor and the implicit power relationship between mentor and trainee. In this section some aspects of this relationship are explored.

When asked what he had enjoyed about mentoring, one male mentor admitted that 'it was good for the ego . . . it's nice to have someone treat you like a deity.' Such a perception suggests that the model of teacher as expert with trainee as apprentice might still exist in the minds of some mentors! Perhaps it is also indicative of the isolation which teachers can feel when their work in the classroom goes unnoticed by their colleagues and when they receive little praise and encouragement.

To be seen as a 'deity' by a trainee does create a problem, however, which may particularly apply to George IV and De Montfort where all the mentors have positions of responsibility. There is a danger that any trainee may see a gap between what they perceive as their own inadequacies and the expertise of the mentor. When that mentor is a high status figure in the school this gap could be even more difficult to bridge.

Some mentors recognise that they need to guard against this and they employ various strategies to display their fallibilities to trainees, such as being very self-critical. One way in which mentors deliberately destroy their own mystique is by engaging with the student in collaborative planning. When trainees observe a lesson they are usually unaware of the extent to which it conforms to the teacher's original plan. One of the many benefits of collaborative planning is that it allows trainees to evaluate how successful a teacher has been in executing intentions. Thus an opportunity is provided to model the reflective practitioner rather than an ideal.

The relationships between mentors interviewed and their trainees appear to be have been close, sometimes almost intense. Many of the mentors interviewed struggled to find words to describe the uniqueness of this rapport: 'You develop a particular relationship with them which is unlike anything else in your job. It's not a pupil-teacher relationship and it's not a colleague-to-colleague set-up.'

Many of the mentors have found that it is this special character of their relationship with the trainees which has contributed to the satisfaction they have experienced in carrying out their role. They do recognise potential problems which may arise, however: issues relating to professionalism and loyalty were raised by several mentors. The relationship which develops would almost seem to encourage confidences to be revealed and three mentors admitted discussing colleagues with their trainees: 'I sound off to the student, which could land me in trouble if the relationship deteriorated.'

Menter points out that trainees are aware from the outset that they are in a weak position relative to the mentor, who they know will carry the major responsibility for their assessment. The comments of one mature female trainee reflect this:

> Survival was imperative and avoiding confrontation [with the mentor] became so ingrained that assertive interaction and the possibility of development were destroyed . . . You want to do the best you can for your own self-esteem but you also want to please your mentor, the kids, the university and your partner (by not spending all your evenings working!). You see your mentor as a guide, friend, counsellor, model, boss, assessor . . . need I go on?

This is a problem inherent in a system by which a mentor is both assessor and supporter. Lacey recognises that if the trainees unburden themselves to the person who is in many respects most able to help, they risk revealing the true depth of their difficulties and demonstrate that they are unable to get by. Some mentors overcome this by making a close, affective relationship with their student and jettisoning the assessor role.

> But for those who attempt both a close relationship and an assessor role the dilemma is deepened. The close relationship with the student, if successful, releases the student from his bind and he openly confesses to his difficulties . . . If the student's difficulties continue the tutor reaches the point where he feels he has a duty to report these difficulties and the student is 'at risk'. From the student's perspective this reversal of his tutor's role seems like a betrayal.
>
> (Lacey, 1977, p. 88)

One female trainee described a situation which illustrates this problem:

> I was having dreadful times at home and it really was affecting my performance in school. I felt that I couldn't tell my mentor because I didn't want him to have to make excuses for me . . . I had so many different roles. One moment we were clashing over sexual politics and the next he was telling me about both his girlfriends. It got too personal – if someone is telling you their problems one minute and coming the heavy

professional the next it's difficult to take. I became a sort of mother figure
. . . he even asked me to carry his books to his car. I didn't know what to
say. This person was going to write a report on me . . .

GENDER AND AGE

Many of the interviewees made comments which would seem to indicate
that there are areas worthy of exploration relating to how trainees perceive
themselves and are perceived according to their gender.

A male mentor spoke about a meeting which he had attended at the
university at which mentors had been invited to comment briefly on their
trainee's progress. He had noticed that mentors of both sexes considered
that the female trainees were generally hard working, thorough and well
prepared, whilst the male trainees appeared to sometimes 'get by with scant
lesson preparation and were more laid back'.

Another male mentor was aware that the dominance which his role as a
mentor gave him was potentially strengthened when his trainee was female
and he found this uncomfortable.

Two female trainees commented on a lack of self-confidence displayed by
many women students and that the male trainees 'could get away with patchy
attendance at university, scruffy appearance at school and deficient course
files'. One female trainee admitted feeling rather bitter about this, especially
as some of the women on the course had not yet found teaching posts but
the men had. This particular trainee had been placed in a department with
a male trainee and she said that there had been a discrepancy in the way in
which they had been assessed, the female trainee being judged against more
rigorous criteria than her male counterpart. Although they had both received
positive reports, she felt his was undeserved. There are obviously many other
factors which might lie behind this case, but the significance lies in the fact
that the trainee perceives the situation in terms of gender.

Another female trainee was concerned that self-evaluation disadvantages
women: 'All the women write terrible things about themselves and all the
men think that they are brilliant . . . Women are taught to be self-deprecating
and will therefore be harder on themselves.'

As with gender issues, very little exploration has been conducted into mentor/
trainee relationships which consider age differences between the parties. One
should not assume that the traditional model of mature mentor and young
trainee still holds. Not only does the Sussex course take a number of mature
students, but mentors are sometimes junior members of the department.
Although the latter is not the case at George IV, three trainees in the last
two years have been over 30 and there have been two instances where male
mentors in their 30s have been responsible for female trainees in their 40s.
Four of the six trainees interviewed were over 25.

A general view expressed by the mentors interviewed was that older students tended to lack confidence initially and needed more support. One student, herself in her 40s, offered an explanation for this which summed up several similar responses:

> The expectation which mature students have of themselves is more pronounced. They are doing the course for some reason outside of simply finding a job; they are doing it for some reason to do with their identity. They are re-training for something after quite a long time of doing something else. Some have broken up relationships. This is their chance to become independent and so it's important. It's their whole life and identity on the line, not just whether they get a teaching job, so they do take it seriously.

This powerful comment is given an added poignancy when it appears that mature female trainees are not finding it easy to acquire teaching posts at the current time. Some awareness that older students *do* experience concerns of a different nature needs to be displayed by mentors in their dealings with trainees.

THE BENEFITS OF MENTORING

All the mentors in both primary and secondary schools have enjoyed the experience and felt that they have learned from it. Trainees brought new ideas about their subject and how to teach it. Mentors said that they frequently have to re-think their own teaching methods in order to explain them to the trainees. They have learned about the nature of teachers and teaching, broadening their repertoire of skills and strategies:

> I've learned that it's still quite difficult to be a teacher . . . Different kinds of teachers have different kinds of problems and different ways of dealing with them.

> Watching her make the mistakes I make.

It has, in some cases, prompted mentors to consider theoretical issues, especially as they see trainees keeping departments in touch with current changes in educational thought and practices. Charting the development of 'their' trainee was also a source of satisfaction:

> I enjoy seeing them flower, when it's largely down to me.

> Nurturing, encouraging and seeing them develop confidence is very pleasing.

Further, and just as importantly, there have been other by-products:

> My listening skills have improved and I think I've learned how to help them [trainees] to see their own strengths and weaknesses.

I've learned transferable skills like interviewing and how to judge people.

I've enjoyed having somebody to talk to about the class.

One primary mentor welcomed the opportunity of doing something other than her usual activities, especially as it allowed her to meet with other mentors, visit other schools and talk to university staff.

A remark by Haggar (in Benton, 1990) referring to the Oxford Internship scheme is perhaps an apt concluding statement for this section:

> Their [the mentors'] enthusiasm for this planned enterprise which entailed considerably more work for them at a time when they were grappling with the demands of the new GCSE examinations and having to face up to the implications of the Education Reform Bill was nothing less than astounding, and suggested that Internship also had much to offer to them and their pupils.
>
> (Benton, 1990, p. 109)

CONCLUSION: THE WAY FORWARD

In an era of imposed change in education it would seem that, at least in the area of initial teacher training, there is scope to be proactive and this research indicates that there are positive aspects of mentoring on which to build. All the mentors interviewed saw strengths in the school-based structure of a course, where a partnership not only prepares trainees to become teachers but also enriches the work of the mentors. Although the DFE criteria impose certain parameters within which the partnership must operate, there is room for the parties involved to be both interpretative and creative.

A whole school approach to mentoring would seem essential if many of the issues raised in this study are to be addressed. The wider school community needs to understand the rationale behind the partnership and the roles played by the various protagonists. At the centre should lie a policy expressing a whole school commitment. It should state what it sees as the aims of its involvement in the partnership and provide a description of roles which suggest who, within the school structure, is best suited to mentoring. I would recommend that the trainees' entitlement should be established by the school, stressing the professional aspects that constitute a wider school experience. The nature of this whole experience offered to trainees should be monitored to ensure that all trainees within a school are afforded similar opportunities. There should be a reiteration of equal opportunities, with reference to teacher training, to raise awareness of gender issues within mentoring. This policy should be related to the school's policies regarding appraisal, newly qualified teachers and staff development so that there is a recognition of common links.

A 'needs audit' could establish the basis for mentor training becoming part of the school's staff development programme. The development of performance indicators to aid in mentor self-appraisal would be a step towards the creation of the self-reflective school.

Training institutions also have a role to play, as they need to develop a mechanism which would provide the feedback which mentors require. The university could also consider ways in which schools can be made aware of the gender and age issues illuminated in this chapter.

Both partners could encourage action research in the field of mentoring. This would provide teachers with a creative role in their professional development which could enhance the quality of their performance. In the absence of the provision of money and large amounts of extra time for mentors, recognition in the form of accreditation for professional qualifications would provide an incentive. This would also encourage teachers to reflect on their practice and become familiar with research methodology and literature relating to teacher training.

Both institutions could join forces in developing packages for training teachers in the generic skills of mentoring such as observation, giving feedback, conflict solving and assessment, which are of use to all teachers as they apply to the education of pupils as well as to that of trainees. It is important in this training to recognise the complex dynamic that exists between trainee and mentor. An approach which tackles the day-to-day realities of mentoring could again be given to schools as a training package for use in staff development programmes.

This chapter suggests that, in general, mentoring is seen in a positive light by all those involved, but there are some problems which will not easily be resolved by the measures suggested above. The suitability of schools and mentors can be monitored by training institutions, local education authorities and OFSTED, but it will still be difficult to ensure consistency in the quality of experiences offered to trainees. Furthermore, the twin needs of money and time must be satisfied if partnership is to be significantly different from the traditional university/school relationship. There is a danger otherwise that 'partnership' will merely signify an extended period in schools where trainees learn to accept and perpetuate a status quo.

8

PRINCIPLED MENTORING AND COMPETENCY-DRIVEN TEACHER EDUCATION IN AN URBAN COMPREHENSIVE SCHOOL

Paul Stephens

This chapter is suggestive rather than definitive, for it is based on the work of one mentor – myself – in a large, mixed, urban comprehensive school during the period September 1993 – July 1994. Moreover, it is written from the standpoint of a 'chalk on the hands' practitioner rather than of a campus academic. It therefore makes fewer references than are customary to published research, but draws abundantly from professional experience.

An important task of the mentor is to provide intending teachers with access to expert knowledge which works in practical situations. This task closely matches the DFE expectation that 'training' should:

> equip students with essential 'competencies', including the subject knowledge and professional and personal skills which new teachers need to manage, maintain order and teach effectively in their classrooms.
>
> (DFE, 1993, p. 4)

The emphasis here on linking training to definable competencies comes fairly easily to mentors. After all, mentoring involves a considerable amount of practical application. The routinising tendencies of DFE directives, however, sit uneasily with university tutors, who generally prefer a less technical, more reflective approach to teacher education.

My chapter argues that this 'tension' offers creative opportunities for campus and school-based teacher educators to provide student teachers with the moral and political vision, and the pedagogical leverage, to become competent and principled practitioners. I assert that competency acquisition should be promoted by initiating student teachers into fairly explicitly defined – but not overly formulaic – professional skills, within a framework of moral and political awareness. In that context student teachers should be encouraged to:

- critically examine, through observation, discussion and role play with university tutors and mentors, the five DFE competencies (subject knowledge, subject application, class management, assessment and recording, and professional development), which 'are designed to ensure that new entrants to the teaching profession are well equipped for their role' (DFE, 1993, p. 1);
- model their performance on the ways in which mentors successfully demonstrate both a repertoire of recognisable competencies and a simultaneous awareness of, and a sensitivity to, wider moral and political issues.

While I give some attention to what goes on in the university components of initial teacher education, I say much more about what happens when student teachers learn and cultivate their professional craft skills and practise their authentic humanity in the school. For the school is where I do my work; it is the place where I seek to persuade student teachers that their intended profession requires both practical strategies and principled aims.

What do I mean by principled, though? I believe that a principled teacher is one who acts on conscience whether or not this coincides with the system. If the teacher and the system are in harmony there is little or no moral strain; when the opposite occurs teachers are faced with a painful choice: to do what they believe to be right even if that means challenging the organisational ethos, or to surrender their principles and become uncritical servants of the wider structure.

I believe that, in my professional work with school students and student teachers, I should be:

- a provider of knowledge and skills;
- an educative and a personal counsellor;
- an opponent of prejudice and discrimination and a champion of equality;
- an advocate and a practitioner of non-coercive class management.

I am not a philosopher, so I will not seek to demonstrate that my definition of 'principled' has access to a higher moral order than that of colleagues who have a different vision. All I can do, is to be explicit about my vision.

BACKGROUND

I am Head of Social Sciences at an 11–19, 1,800 roll, mixed comprehensive school in a large city in the north of England, where I teach A-level sociology.

I work alongside a colleague who teaches A-level law and two colleagues who teach A-level psychology. During the 1993–94 school year I mentored five PGCE students from a nearby university on their secondary school placements. Two students specialised in business and economics, two in history and one in sociology, these placements accounting for two-thirds of the PGCE course. The business and economics, and history students spent most of their classroom time in the departments that teach those subjects; the sociology student honed his skills in my department. All five students met with me for a seventy-minute reflective seminar on a weekly basis.

My school is purpose-built and is located in a predominantly urban, white, working class neighbourhood on the outskirts of the city. The area's former mining heritage is proudly proclaimed by a school tapestry of the area's coal-seamed underbelly. The school takes in students from the immediate environs and from wide outlying districts, including one of the poorest areas of the city.

Today's inhabitants are mainly of 'new working class' stock, more likely to be found in service occupations than in heavy industry. However, there is still a blue-collar feel about the community, reflected in part by the school brass band and the working men's club. Some managerial and professional families reside in the area, but they usually live on private estates and in semi-detached houses. Not so their less well paid neighbours, who generally occupy council estates and two-up, two-down terraces. It is from these families, predominantly urban working class with some clusters of salaried employees, that most of our students are recruited.

In so far as the cultures of the school and the local community coincide, as a teacher, I sense that parents, governors and senior staff want the school to provide a learning and a pastoral environment that supports and sustains:

- a high level of conforming behaviour;
- very firm discipline;
- good public examination results;
- access to higher education;
- little or no truancy;
- regular, rigorously monitored homework;
- success in sporting events.

Although there is a degree of sub-cultural resistance among certain 'progressive' teachers to this official regime, there is quite a lot of organisational pressure on teachers to not rock the boat. In fact, faced with recalcitrant and sometimes aggressive school students during tough substitution periods, I am sometimes tempted to take the line of least resistance by invoking the threat of punishment, although I remain firmly committed to a non-coercive ethos.

Going with the flow – in this case an authoritarian current – is professionally easy. It works because students are inducted, right from day one, into a tightly 'policed' system. Most students conform without manifest protestation; a sizeable minority make loud remonstrations but yield quickly when teachers get tough; a very small number of students accomplish those more subtle but highly effective forms of institutional defiance so vividly captured by Paul Willis, namely, the sustaining of 'an aimless air of insubordination ready with spurious justification and impossible to nail down', (Willis, 1977, p. 13).

Yet survival, from an 'I'm in control' perspective, is not hard to achieve where punitive back-up can almost always be tapped in an institution that believes in sanctions. Even the toughest school students can usually be brought back into line by exposing them to graded steps of increasingly severe punishments, should initial actions fail to elicit appropriate submissiveness. But where does all this lead? Measured against DFE criteria, the tough disciplinarians in my school would score highly on the criteria used for 'competent' class managers, but how would they fare on the more elusive scale of being principled in their work? I cannot answer that question for them. However, I do believe that any teacher who uses sanctions for purely pragmatic purposes, without considering the wider ethical and political implications of this form of social control, is not really coming to grips with the issue of conscientious practice.

As a teacher and as a mentor it is my task to find ways to act on my belief in non-combative styles of class management and to make that expertise available to my student teachers in a regime whose organisational goals are strongly buttressed by a system of sanctions. Yet theirs is the experience of a very different educational setting. When they come to me they swap a tolerant, tree-lined campus in a cathedral city some twenty-five miles away to enter an altogether hardier environment.

INSTITUTIONAL CULTURES

This contrast of surroundings, the one urbane, the other gritty, is complemented to some extent by differing institutional cultures. The campus is able to cultivate a reflective ethos; the school must focus on practicalities. This produces a tension: university tutors expect student teachers to step outside of and deliberate upon the context of mere doing; school mentors are expected to make available to intending teachers the distilled wisdom of craft-professional knowledge.

There is a certain inevitability here. Universities do not usually have school students on site. That gives campus tutors the space and the time to encourage student teachers to ponder the limitations and the promises of scripted classroom strategies. Mentors, by contrast, are dispensers of 'know-how' in classrooms, sports fields, corridors and canteens, and, by DFE decree, assessors of the developing 'competencies' of student teachers where the action is: in the school.

In that context James Calderhead is probably right when he claims that, 'in schools a much higher priority is given to immediate, spontaneous action rather than analysis and reflection' (Calderhead, 1992, p. 2). The institutional cultures of schools are usually geared to day-to-day routines and practical exigencies. Moreover, student teachers expect their mentors to dispense 'off-the-shelf' wisdoms rather than vaguely felt musings.

However, mentors can and, I believe, should resist pressures from whatever quarter to rely simply on 'pat on the shoulder, this is how to do it' advice. When, for example, I discuss with my PGCE students the competencies that explicitly define what the DFE requires me and other providers of initial teacher education to do in respect of 'training' (DFE, 1992), I do not reduce my counsel to a list of 'teacher should . . .' directives. We also consider issues that are not always amenable to learning outcome audits prescribed by invisible 'experts' in a distant government department, issues like how important it is to give school students the right to get angry during a heated classroom debate, instead of automatically invoking 'appropriate sanctions' (DFE, 1992, 2.4.3). In this reflective work I am fully supported by my co-teacher educators at the university. They recognise the inevitability of a certain division of labour between mentors and tutors, but they also realise that, despite the faster tempo of chalkface practice, what goes on in schools is much more than just shooting from the hip. Teachers are thinkers as well as doers, and the most efficacious doers think before they act.

Given the practical setting in which I work, I do try to translate the minutiae of DFE legalese into bold outline descriptions and practical strategies. But I need also to make student teachers aware that being a teacher means much more than successfully demonstrating an inventory of pre-specified competencies. Otherwise, mentors like me risk turning out the kind of newly qualified teacher who, as David Carr puts it, 'may perform routinely well according to the lights or the behest of others rather than on the basis of her own principled understanding'. (Carr, 1993, p. 262).

I will illustrate this point with reference to some real mentoring, specifically how I respond, in work with student teachers, to the DFE competency criteria on class management. The official criteria employ the language of control: 'decide when', 'create', 'devise and use', 'maintain'. There are also references to 'orderly environments' and 'appropriate rewards and sanctions' (DFE, 1992, 2.4). Such state-mandated vocabulary is not at odds with what my school expects of its teachers. But it is at odds with my perception of principled teaching and principled mentoring.

In seminars with my PGCE students I encourage them to consider the extent to which their own beliefs and values align with the official agenda of DFE directives and school practice. But this does not mean substituting whimsical diversions for the real business of getting these intending teachers properly prepared for work in the classroom. Like me, they know that they must display visible competency in the way they make complex tasks achievable for all their students, in the way they utilise individual, group and whole class teaching to good effect, and in the way they take account of psychological and social factors in the assessment of learning outcomes.

All of these skills are 'permitted' by DFE Circular 9/92, and all of them require considerable prior reflection and discussion. Moreover, such competencies are not merely reducible to a scripted list of behavioural responses. Competent teachers are contextual experts. They have become adept at identifying particular cues – the procedural discipline of the laboratory, the impromptu incident in the playground – and, almost effortlessly it seems, taking the appropriate course of action. Competent teachers are also disposed to look beyond the immediacy of the next lesson. In that sense they apply competencies thoughtfully and relevantly, and plan ahead.

When mentors and other experienced teachers seek to make what they do so routinely and so effectively in schools accessible to student teachers, they need to make their receptivity to background contingencies and their long-term strategies explicit. This might mean, for example, explaining to an intending teacher that regional dialects in the classroom should not be considered inferior to so-called standard English. In that context it would be appropriate to point out that sociological research has documented the damaging effects upon self-esteem and learning outcomes when school students are made to leave their culture (of which a dialect is an important part) at the school gate. There is the important issue too of encouraging intending teachers to adopt a principled attitude here: of showing that they respect and welcome cultural diversity.

It is also relevant, during discussions between mentors and student teachers, to consider and debate the relative merits of different class management styles. At the two extremes of the continuum are coercive management and non-coercive management. In between are varying degrees of control and facilitative strategies. Student teachers need to know that some teachers are selective, employing the method that, in their judgement, best fits the particular circumstance, while others are predominantly coercive or non-coercive, whatever the situation.

From a principled perspective it is necessary to extend the discussion into wider political and ethical domains. Is it the proper role of the teacher in society to frighten students into subservient acceptance of an adult point of view? Is it morally acceptable for the teacher to place organisational imperatives before principled class management? These are important questions. They must not be sidestepped. Nor should mentors urge pragmatism by using expressions like 'it's right not to use intimidation, but in practice you need to stamp your authority rather forcefully, easing off when students start showing you respect'.

I make sure that my student teachers get to watch teachers who live by a different code in action, teachers who cheer when a school student throws a spitball in defence of a spirited argument. Such teachers are not only to be found in Summerhill. They exist in urban comprehensive schools like my own, courageously helping their students to stand by what they believe in, even if that means saying 'no' in the company of a teacher. For there are different ways of saying 'no'. There is the refusal that is premised on the honest rebuttal of an idea, and the refusal that defiantly attacks the authority of a teacher. Principled teachers know this distinction.

It is also necessary to give student teachers the opportunity to observe and to try their hand at those aspects of class management that require even the most 'progressive' of teachers to take a lead in their dealings with school students. Bearing in mind that classes do not just occupy classrooms, but also move around the wider environs of the school, I extend this 'look and have a go' exercise to corridors and bus bays, both of which, for health and safety reasons, require adult supervision.

At the same time, I emphasise, in discussion and by example, that class management, both from a principled and an effective stand-point, should be based on non-coercive practice. Conscientious mentors who know that the DFE wants them to turn out 'carrot and stick' class managers are faced with a difficult choice: to preach and practise the time-honoured 'Start out tough, ease up later' maxim, or to adopt and encourage a 'Start kind, stay kind' approach.

My preference is decidedly for the second of these two options. Not only do I tell my PGCE students that this style of class management allows me to remain honest to my belief in non-coercive practice, I also point out that my professional work and the findings of research DES, 1989) suggest it is a style that works well in real classroom situations. In short, my approach is not simply a matter of personal, idiosyncratic preference; it is premised on experience and evidence.

Does, though, the institutional culture of the school permit the same degree of humanity as the more detached, progressive ethos of the university? This is an issue that I have to deal with in every aspect of my mentoring work. My co-teacher educators at the university appear to – and perhaps do – have the upper hand in the matter of encouraging student teachers to practise justice in the classroom. Unlike me they do not have to contend with the 'don't mess with me' outlook of certain teachers who maintain that showing compassion towards 'difficult' school students displays weakness rather than decency. Such an outlook can easily become the dominant control culture of a school, especially if it is promoted and supported by senior staff. This view can also lend credence to that dangerous juxtaposition which suggests that schools deal with real issues and universities merely conject.

However, teachers can and should resist organisational pressures to conform to beliefs and concomitant practices in which they have little or no faith. It is important, though, to engage in resistance that neither rebukes custodial-minded colleagues, nor which confuses students with avant-garde messages that sit uneasily within the strictures of a rather formal regime. Discussing this tension with PGCE students is all part of the process of encouraging reflective practice.

TEACHERS ARE REFLECTIVE TOO

It is fashionable these days for academics to urge schoolteachers to become reflective practitioners. One detects, in this admonition, an assumption on the part of our campus counterparts that we teachers are so overwhelmed by contemporary pressures, like the spiralling rise in truancy rates and the impersonal staccato of centrally prescribed assessment procedures, that we have lost our idealism. I hope that such is not the case. There are still teachers, schools and education authorities who conscientiously struggle against prejudice and injustice, who strive to give all their students a thorough educational and an ethical preparation for the world in and beyond the classroom. When, for example, education authorities like my own produce written policies on equal opportunities, schools and teachers are expected to reflect on the implications, as well as acting on the principles of such initiatives.

Illustrative of that point, I recently invited two council officials who have a special interest in women's issues into my classroom. They explained to me and my students how routine practices in schools and elsewhere are often gendered in ways that work against girls and women. Their presentations elicited a lot of critical discussion and have encouraged us to be much more ready than hitherto to challenge sexism. I have also spoken to other teachers in my school about the ways in which they have consistently developed practical strategies, premised on a great deal of constructive reflection, for confronting gendered prejudices and for helping students to eradicate sexist assumptions from their daily lives.

Moreover, as a mentor I send copies of my department's mission statement to student teachers before they begin their school-based programme. This document states explicitly where I and my colleagues stand on issues that are crucially linked to principled professional practice. For example, the document makes it clear that the department is committed to:

> Encouraging and enabling you [the school student] to base your studies and your moral and citizenship outlook on objective, anti-ageist, anti-racist and anti-sexist criteria. If we [the teachers] manage to replace any negative 'ism' with an enlightened, generous outlook, any hearsay judgement with critical awareness, any half-truth with honest scholarship, then we will have done our job well.

Statements like this are not intended to produce knee-jerk responses to unexpected events; rather, the opposite. Their purpose is to promote critical reflection and responsible teaching. Moreover, the above statement did not just jump onto a page. It was considered, discussed, refined and eventually written with a long-term goal in mind: to cultivate in our students an ability and a readiness to identify and challenge those attitudes and practices in society that undermine equality and social justice.

Further indicative of reflective work on the part of teachers is the burgeoning growth of practitioner-led research in schools, often linked to school improvement programmes. In this area I have initiated research into those aspects of initial teacher education that student teachers report most help them to acquire and augment DFE competence 2.4: class management skills. This research involves collaboration with academics at the university, who provide expert advice and guidance on methods and data interpretation.

However, the project is conducted by two teachers, myself and a colleague, and, like many other teachers, we are crossing the traditional dividing line between chalkface and campus cultures. Not only are we engaged in reflective research whose findings will, hopefully, help to turn out good class managers, we are also getting our student teachers to do a lot of hard reflecting themselves. Out of a series of informal interviews and some questionnaires, important and interesting findings are emerging.

In our case study student teachers report that class management styles are:

- Best introduced and considered on campus prior to school placement, through the use of videos, role play and seminar-style discussion.
- Quite clearly linked to specific subjects (more emphasis on hierarchical command structures are deemed necessary in science practicals, for example, than in discursive humanities classes).
- Closely related to overarching institutional cultures (my school is seen as tough on discipline, and student teachers feel they are expected to fall in line with that ethos, whether or not this sits easily with their own preferred style).
- Very effectively learnt, in practical terms, through the observation of skilled teachers who put on rather stylised, almost scripted, demonstrations that are accompanied by follow-up discussions with the demonstrators and 'have a go yourself' practice.

Admittedly the research is suggestive rather than representative. That said, it tentatively questions the notion that class management is merely a technical skill whose accomplishment is simply developed by 'watch and do' activities in classrooms. To be sure, that aspect plays an important part, but student teachers also see a need for reflective work and for discussions about how their private moralities interact with DFE and public expectations regarding the teacher's role as disciplinarian.

They also need to be given opportunities to engage in principled practice during initial teacher education. I know this might seem rather idealistic, given that some 'old hands' have an irritating tendency to tell student teachers that school students deal soft-touch beginners a tough hand. Yet, in my experience, most school students have an impeccable sense of fair play, and they respond most affably and most productively when they recognise the same quality in their teachers. In that spirit, and supported by the evidence of my own practitioner research, as well as by the published research of university academics (e.g. Brown and McIntyre, 1993; Wragg, 1993), I advise student teachers, for ethical and practical reasons, to demonstrate qualities that school students say they appreciate:

- displaying a sense of humour without being ridiculously jolly;
- avoiding condescending remarks and rebuffs at all costs;
- showing patience when a class or an individual gets stuck;
- demonstrating that they know their stuff;
- having a lot of enthusiasm for their subject;
- being caring, kind and sympathetic;
- making complex issues understandable;
- adopting firmness when things get out of hand;
- maintaining fairness and integrity when adjudicating disputes.

In dispensing this guidance I recognise that my student teachers are becoming not just exponents of a craft, but members of a caring profession. They need both competencies and moral purpose. The DFE puts far too much emphasis on the skills side of things, but a careful reading of its criteria reveals that a sensitivity to the differing learning and personal needs of school students is also necessary. Would that the DFE gave such pastoral awareness more of a focus. However, that does not stop mentors nor university tutors from giving foremost attention in teacher education to the caring work upon which principled practice is premised.

Campus educators use lectures, seminars, tutorials and workshops to deal with the ethics and the politics of the teacher's role. We mentors employ some of those methods, but we also bring the debate into real professional work. In that context I find one of the best ways to make student teachers aware that this authentic labour has both reflective and craft dimensions is to move the school-based experiences of student teachers beyond the routines of classrooms, corridors and gym halls into the decision-making arenas that are also an integral part of school life.

An excellent way to do this is to have student teachers shadow experienced teachers at heads of department sessions, working party conferences, staff meetings and governors' meetings. These gatherings provide important opportunities to observe vigorous and lively debates that throw into relief the harmonies and the tensions which emerge when individuals and social structures lock horns on ethical and political matters. I like to think of such occasions as forums for the disclosure of creative conflict within real institutional settings. They are social encounters that should not be off limits to intending teachers; this is because they create agendas which force a great deal of reflection. In that respect, they also remind all teachers that what goes on in schools is not confined to check-lists of competencies.

For that is the risk engendered in a preoccupation with the identification and assessment of explicitly defined criteria. Put simply, there are some qualities in the making of good teachers that cannot be squeezed into a competency profile. Indeed, as Ian Davies and Ernesto Macaro so rightly remark, 'it would be possible for a student [teacher] to do well against all competence statements and yet still be regarded as a poor teacher' (Davies and Macaro, 1995, p. 4).

There is something about principled practice that is just not amenable to learning the ropes. No mentor wants to help create a teacher who knows how to put on an ethical show but who is not moved by a conscientious desire to put compassion above organisational imperatives. The best that mentors can do is to nurture those very qualities that coercive school regimes seek to undermine: remaining courteous when relating to school students (even if they are not being the slightest bit courteous themselves); starting out and staying kind and recognising that there is nothing weak about this; and flushing out those aspects of the hidden curriculum that obstruct equal opportunities for black students, students who are disabled, female students and working class students.

With these ends in mind, mentors like myself need to supplement their advice on how to accomplish DFE-prescribed competencies with independent and creative discussions on the nature and the practice of principled teaching. Only then will we be able to help tomorrow's teachers to develop that ingenuity and conviction which enables them to do much more than being merely competent. We will assist them in becoming professionals who take the time to care about what they do and, above all, who make the decision to care about their students.

CONCLUSION

In this chapter I have argued that competency-led initial teacher education should be infused with opportunities for the consideration and practice of principled teaching. I have also made it clear that, in my role as a mentor, I have sought to encourage student teachers to examine critically the ways in which their professional duties are defined and supported by institutional arrangements. Where there is harmony of moral and political purpose between the individual and the school, that represents an almost perfect situation. But where such is not the case, I believe it is important for mentors to show intending teachers, through reflective discussion and conscientious action, that there is a principled way forward.

The socialisation of intending and newly qualified teachers into a professional teaching culture need not be at odds with the idealism more usually associated with campus culture. There is no inevitability of a 'wash-out' effect, whereby mentors purge compassion and replace it with pragmatic 'realism'. For what is real can and should be infused with moral and political purpose. Many of my professional colleagues know and live by that belief. Some of them, to be sure, are forced to fight for their idealism when, for example, they work in schools where enterprise culture has sought to hijack a commitment to public service. But, ultimately, teachers are in part responsible for the normative structures in which they do their work. They should not surrender their convictions to a system in which they do not believe. Instead, in collaboration with like-minded colleagues and through their own professional practice, they should seek to change the system. Principled practice demands nothing less.

9

THE DEVELOPMENT OF A SCHOOL-BASED INITIAL TEACHER TRAINING AND MENTOR SUPPORT PROGRAMME

Janice Windsor

The South Coast Community School is an 11-to-18 mixed comprehensive of 1,550 pupils and 130 staff, 100 of whom are teachers. It has a mixed catchment area, drawing its pupils from a number of outlying rural locations as well as from the expanding seaside town itself. It is truly comprehensive in that it caters for children from the widest variety of backgrounds and abilities.

Like teachers in many schools, we at South Coast have worked with initial teacher training (ITT) students for a considerable number of years. In the past, the school's major role in ITT was to provide teaching practice for the students according to the instructions of the training institution. Students came for their school practice, were attached to classroom teachers who wrote their reports at the end of the practice, and that was an end to it. Sometimes useful discussions took place between the classroom teacher and the college or university tutor, and sometimes good links developed between school and college staff with teaching exchanges taking place. However, these links and experiences were inconsistent, and varied according to the individuals concerned; the school had little say in any important decisions and even less idea about the whole training of the students placed with them. The major responsibility was considered to be with the training institution, and it was assumed by those involved in this school-based component of initial teacher education that all professional and training issues were dealt with by the institution.

The students' periods of teaching practice were traditionally co-ordinated by a senior member of staff – in our school by a deputy head – and the quality of the experience gained by students largely depended on the commitment of individual subject teachers and the amount of time they were able to give to the student during break times and after school. Thus the amount of input from the school to individual ITT students' experience – especially within subject departments – tended to be rather variable and random. This undoubtedly followed the general contemporary pattern for teaching practice provision: '. . . the time devoted to training by teacher tutors and others was frequently left very much to individual teachers and frequently reflected their varying assessment as to what exactly was expected of them . . .' (Furlong, Hirst *et al.*, 1988, p. 191)

When the job of co-ordinating the school practices became part of my role as assistant deputy head we were working with two HEIs which were sending students to us from one-year, two-year and four-year Bachelor of Education (BEd.) courses as well as from PGCE courses. Co-ordinating the practices for all these different teacher training courses in English, mathematics, history, physical education, art, business studies and technology was a very complex business because not only did the two institutions have different term dates, requirements and methods, but departments and courses within the individual institutions differed with regard to 'block practices' and 'serial practices'. We had a situation where, for example, the mathematics department at South Coast would be trying to provide classes for a four-year BEd. student on a block practice in the autumn and spring terms which overlapped with serial practices of one day a week followed by block practices for PGCE students. This put a strain on the school and the departments as well as causing a lack of continuity for both student teachers and pupils. Teachers were often left feeling they had to 'pick up the pieces' following a student's school placement experience; having to organise and debrief both the student's work and that of the rest of the department and the pupils affected by the placement, without any very clear idea of when and how the next placement might be arranged.

When we at South Coast Community School were originally invited to join the Sussex University Secondary PGCE partnership by providing training places for geography, science, modern languages and music ITT students, we initially saw this primarily as an opportunity to help us to recruit good members of staff in the shortage subjects at the end of the course. However, working with the Sussex scheme was to introduce us to a different method of training new teachers by placing greater responsibility on the school.

Our involvement with the Sussex University PGCE pre-dated the government-initiated changes and greater standardisation of PGCE courses which began to occur during the early 1990s, culminating in the publication of circular 9/92. At this point, therefore, the course was designed so that the trainees remained with one school for the major part of the teaching experience followed by a shorter 'professional development' placement. This did not have to take place in a school setting, and could be linked to work in a wider educational field generally chosen by the trainee – for example in museum education work, various forms of special education, or in field study centres.

Under the arrangements laid down by the Sussex scheme the school was expected to take a more active role in the training and provide a mentor for each student from the relevant subject department. In return a small fee was paid to the school for each trainee placed with us.

We found that the practice of retaining the same ITT students from October until Easter produced a greater feeling of commitment in the school to their training and we began to examine the quality of what we were offering. I became the professional tutor, with a responsibility for overseeing the school-based experience of all the Sussex PGCE students placed with us, and in accordance with the expectations of the University the system of mentorship as required under the Sussex scheme was established.

I began my work in this new role by holding weekly seminars with the students from Sussex as well as tutorials during the school lunch breaks. Subject mentors were fitting in their departmental-based sessions with the students as and when they could. When students from the other institutions with whom we had links were in school during periods of teaching practice they joined the weekly professional tutor seminars and there were frequent positive comments about the value of sharing ideas and experiences across the training institutions.

Then came government circular 9/92 (DFE, 1992) and the prospect of funding for the schools in return for firm commitment to involvement in school-based initial teacher training. It was clear that under the new arrangements the schools were going to have to take a major responsibility in the training of new teachers, and we felt that the supporting structure we had begun to develop now needed to become more formal in order to give it status and permanence. As Barbara Field asserts:

> With an initial teacher education program that is two thirds school-based, provision has to be made in the school's side of the partnership, as well as in the university's side, for the theory/practice link to be made . . . The *practicum* must now become a systematic programmed teaching of all aspects of classroom teaching, not only a socialisation into the school 'society' and into the technical and craft skills needed for survival in the classroom.
>
> (Field and Field, 1994, pp. 63–4)

RESPONSES TO CIRCULAR 9/92

It is my belief that the key to the success of any form of ITT in a school, and particularly of the scale of organisation and involvement required of schools by 9/92, depends largely on the status which that school is prepared to give to it. In the South Coast Community School teacher training has achieved a high status. This is due to a number of factors: namely the wholehearted commitment to ITT of the headteacher, senior management team and professional tutor as well as the involvement of an enthusiastic and dedicated team of mentors who have the credibility and respect of their colleagues. Teachers in this school began to see the development and career opportunities which could arise from participation in ITT. They could also see the importance placed on it by senior colleagues. That such a perception is crucial to the success of school-based initial teacher training has been widely recognised (Beck and Booth 1992, and Kelly, Beck and ap Thomas in Wilkin, 1992, pp. 30–4 and 173–80; Evans in Wilkin and Sankey, 1994, p. 64–5).

As with all innovations and decisions to commit the school to specific course(s) of action, approval and interest clearly signalled by those in senior and influential posts in the school greatly enhanced the chances for success. At the outset it was clear to the headteacher and professional tutor that the increased importance of the role of the school in the training of teachers had the potential for bringing many overall advantages to the school. It would assist in lifting the professional self-esteem of the staff, help with the recruitment of good teachers and ensure that we were constantly reviewing our own craft in the classroom. Opportunities for increased levels of professional development of all staff would thus be considerably enhanced by this decision to give wholehearted support to greater involvement in school-based ITT.

The enthusiasm of the headteacher and professional tutor persuaded the senior management team that in order to prepare for compliance with 9/92 it would be worthwhile timetabling the periods necessary for subject mentors to work specifically with ITT students, regardless of the level of funding available to cover such an allocation of teacher time being provided by individual HEIs. Designating and protecting such mentor time was a key factor in proving to colleagues that here was a serious and lasting new development; a development which would beneficially affect the status of a school hoping eventually to become a training school. Obvious comparisons might be made with the standing of a training hospital in providing a centre of excellence for the development and nurture of the next generation of professionals.

The support for this requirement of specifically assigned time to be made available for ITT work came from the expectation of Sussex University that there should be a mentor period of at least one hour per week per student in order to qualify for funding within the post-9/92 arrangements put into place for the University's partnership with schools, under which PGCE students were to receive their 'hands-on' classroom experience. It was thought by us to be most important that this protected, non-classroom teaching time should not be regarded as a kind of 'perk', providing an additional non-contact period for mentors, but should be shown on the whole school timetable as a teaching commitment.

As professional tutor I was also timetabled to deliver seminars on whole school issues to the cohort of ITT students placed with us; to carry out and report on classroom-based observation of students; and to give individual students tutorial time. The importance of my commitment, in my role as professional tutor to the school's overall ITT programme, was further acknowledged through the timetabling of my workload so as to incorporate recognition of the considerable amount of administration and correspondence involved in school-based ITT work, as well as to provide time for me to arrange for and implement the monitoring of the whole programme.

After some discussion with the schools' information and management systems (SIMS) manager, it was decided that the entire allocation of mentor and professional tutor sessions should be shown on the whole school timetable as 'Year 14'.

Providing ITT for adults also fitted in with implementation of our explicit philosophy of the Community School having responsibility for provision of education across all stages of life 'from the cradle to the grave' (we had recently opened a nursery and pre-school unit under the auspices of the Community School). Thus ITT became part of the acknowledged and essential curriculum being offered by the school, and the mentors felt that the job they were doing was receiving real recognition, and was fundamental to the school's operation and vision of itself as a provider of education to the whole community. (See also Sayer, 1989, p. 62, for further comments on this.)

Initial teacher training becoming part of the curriculum of the school naturally led to the expectation that programmes of study would be developed for the successful delivery of ITT, as in all other aspects of the school's curriculum provision. Mentors produced their own subject induction and study programmes, to be followed by the students allocated to their departments. It was felt that these schemes of work, although carefully structured to provide a thorough grounding in subject application, classroom management and other relevant professional competences, had to have some built-in elements of flexibility in order to meet the needs of individual trainee teachers.

Each week a seminar on whole school issues was arranged and led by the professional tutor. All ITT students currently within the school were expected to take part. The style of these seminars varied between discussion, role play and lectures. Other teaching colleagues from within the school and representatives from outside agencies were also asked to participate (for example from the Education Welfare Service, from the local advisory teams or governors).

The size of the group of trainee teachers varied according to the school practice dates of individual HEIs, but generally speaking all three of those from whom ITT students were placed in the school were represented. Only the students from Sussex University were able to benefit from the full year's programme however, because of the length of their school practice which covered the greater part of the autumn and the whole of the spring terms. The programme concentrated on professional and whole school issues. For example, one week we would be role-playing a parents' consultation evening in preparation for the students' participation in an actual experience of such an event; another week we might be exploring body language in the classroom or examining the concept of community education. At the beginning of the spring term each student was prepared for job applications by a briefing given by the headteacher followed by a mock interview and de-brief with a member of the senior management team. The evaluations of this professional tutor programme, given by the ITT students at the end of their time in school, showed a positive reaction to the programme, particularly in respect of the assistance and guidance given with finding their first teaching posts.

DEVELOPING THE INVOLVEMENT OF THE MENTOR TEAM

When circular 9/92 was published and the new arrangements for school-HEI partnership and delivery of ITT were laid down, we felt confident that our existing programme could develop, but three things had to be done. We had to develop a whole school policy on initial teacher training, improve the quality of what we were already offering and train new mentors within specific subject departments. These three things sat easily together. Who better to develop the policy than the mentors? Developing a policy would involve discussion, as with any new school policy; discussion involved training. (Dean, 1991 passim)

Mentor training for working with newly qualified teachers (NQTs) and licensed teachers had already been offered to schools such as ours by the local authority and by HEIs, but problems with funding and the difficulties and expense incurred to the whole school in providing cover for up to eight mentors at a time meant that only a small number of teachers could attend such training sessions. It therefore seemed logical that we should provide our own in-house training at the same time as developing our policy and provision for school-based ITT. We felt it to be most important that our students should have a consistent quality of experience, so the professional tutor formed a core team from existing, experienced mentors. Meetings were arranged for this team on a fortnightly basis in order to discuss how we could formulate common policies across the school with regard to such issues as:

- the work required of teachers taking up a mentor's role;
- our expectations of students as members of the school community;
- classroom observation;
- how to tackle the writing of reports;
- ways of coping with the tension which exists for mentors and others involved with teacher trainees in school (as well as for the professional tutor);
- the tension between being supportive to students on the one hand and fulfilling in a professional way the need to assess on the other.

At the same time these fortnightly meetings developed into a forum where we were able to share ideas among ourselves about our programmes of study for ITT students within individual subject departments, as well as pooling news on the latest developments regarding ITT coming from our respective partner institutions. These meetings took place at lunch times and the pill of necessary attendance at them during mentors' precious 'free time' was sweetened through the provision of lunch for those taking part from the school's in-service training

(INSET) budget. The fact that the professional tutor is also in charge of staff training and the budget helped too!

These lunchtime meetings were very much a team affair with the usual format being the presentation of a paper relating to one or other of the issues outlined above by one of the mentors, who then led a general discussion on specific proposals. Following discussion and quite possibly amendment, decisions as to the adoption of specific policies were made at a subsequent meeting after the team had had sufficient time to consider the proposals and very often to discuss them with colleagues within the same subject department, who would also be likely to be affected. This method of development ensured the shared ownership of the policy and programme for ITT within the school among those who were to be responsible for its successful implementation.

As the idea of mentoring caught on in the school, the competition to become a mentor increased. Teachers saw it as a very valuable stage in their own professional development as well as opening up a possible career path for the future.

In its discussions on the role and selection of mentors, the team had decided the criteria which it was felt should be used. These included such qualities as providing a good role model for aspiring teachers, and having good organisational skills in order to be able to cope effectively with the inevitable extra work load as well as being approachable. This meant that being selected as a mentor came to be regarded as a step up on the career ladder, an acknowledgement of valuable skills and the ability to make an important contribution, thus increasing the status of the position. When the opportunity for appointing new mentors arose we were faced with the situation that more than one member of a subject faculty expressed the wish to become involved. This meant that we had to reconsider our methods for appointing mentors.

In the past it had been left to the heads of departments to nominate the mentor following an informal discussion with the candidate within the department. Now it was felt that, with the new status given to mentors and the eagerness with which potential candidates approached the role, the decision must be made at a higher level. The headteacher, after discussion with the professional tutor and the head of faculty, now began to appoint all new mentors. However, the mentor team had been involved in the decision to set up this new application and appointment structure. The problem had been put to them and the subsequent discussion of the issues involved was a valuable training exercise in itself. It may be that as the role of the school in the training of new teachers develops even further this current system of nominating and recruiting new mentors may have to be reconsidered yet again.

There was also a written outcome of the work of the mentor team. We felt that we ought to produce a booklet especially for students. It had been the practice to give students a copy of the staff handbook issued to all teachers working in the Community School – a weighty tome as well as expensive –

but we decided that we should provide ITT trainees with something which was geared towards their particular needs. The writing and production of the booklet was co-ordinated by the professional tutor with mentors contributing specific sections which had been written following the discussions of the whole group concerned with the design and delivery of ITT within the school. In terms of staff development there were spin-offs; mentors were subsequently inspired to produce their own departmental handbooks for students, and to share ideas and practices with colleagues.

As the in-house ITT team began to formulate its policy and practice and to discuss wider issues arising from the school's involvement in ITT, it was felt that this could also be presented in a booklet covering the whole topic of ITT at South Coast, which would be useful not only to the existing mentors, but also to new mentors joining the team and to other interested parties outside the team. We also reasoned that it would probably only be a matter of time before we would be asked to present our policy on the training of students to the governors so we might as well seize the initiative. Our mentor booklet therefore included:

- the school's rationale for being involved in the training of new teachers;
- an outline of the aims and management of the programme;
- discussion of the roles of those involved;
- and guidelines for the successful introduction of various processes which had been developed to enhance and consolidate the experience of ITT students in school, such as the pastoral training of student teachers, successful classroom observation and help with report writing.

It was at this stage with the issue of the mentor booklet that the institutions of higher education from which we accepted students had begun to have serious discussions with schools about the new developments in ITT initiated by the Department for Education and encapsulated in 9/92. At these meetings we were able to share some of our experiences and ideas with colleagues from other schools as well as with tutors from the HEIs. Being involved in the meetings themselves added to the job satisfaction of the mentors and the professional tutor. To be associated with the shaping of a new era in teacher training, and to be in closer contact with colleagues from universities, further added to the status which mentors felt was being accorded to their role as key personnel in the development of a successful programme for the training of a new generation of teachers.

Mentoring can be a very lonely business, and all of us involved have found it of great benefit to share concerns and ideas with each other on a regular basis. There were still many issues to discuss and develop. We needed to clarify the application of the teaching competences listed in 9/92 to our programme, to develop a system of profiling, and to consider such issues as the language we use with student teachers and the counselling role of the mentor.

One of the main thrusts of our agenda following the initial phase of successful establishment of the programme was an examination of the role of classroom teachers who are not mentors working with ITT students. In any large school a mentor will have to arrange for the student teacher to work with a number of colleagues from the same department and quite possibly from others. Ask any students and they will tell you that their practice can quite easily be made or marred by the support and attitudes of the classroom teacher with whom they are placed and who is 'outside' the mentoring relationship, having maybe a quite different understanding of what the nature of a teaching placement should be.

We also have to maintain the quality of lessons being delivered to our pupils. Some teachers have expressed their concerns about meeting the demands of the National Curriculum when they are not seeing their pupils for long periods of time because classes are being taken by trainee teachers. Parents and other interested parties may also express concerns about whether a protracted in-put by students in the classroom might have an adverse effect on the pupils' learning which is taking place.

In our school we decided that part of the answer is that no longer can classroom teachers hand over classes to students and go off to do some marking ... as if they ever did! Now the student and teacher must plan together, team teach sometimes, and each be so well informed about what the other is doing that they can hand over at any time in full knowledge of what has been covered and what needs to be done. The classroom teacher must still be fully responsible for what is being delivered to the pupils. Inevitably, tensions may arise between the needs of the student and the needs of the pupils and it will take a lot of skill on the part of the mentors to choose wisely those teachers with whose classes they intend to place ITT students, negotiate with them what is to be offered to the students and what is to be delivered to the pupils, and to solve the problems which will almost inevitably arise. To this end we, as a working group of mentors, have examined the whole concept of collaborative teaching with ITT students and have drawn up guidelines for all colleagues involved. Training colleagues will not be an easy task for the mentors – there are still a lot of old notions around about what it means to have an ITT student in the classroom and about what should be the obligations of qualified teachers in this situation.

Mentors will need to feel confident and well supported if school-based ITT is to be the successful enterprise that it should, and this brings me back to my original point about the vital importance to all involved of developing the mutual support and reassurance which comes from working closely in a team and with the professional tutor.

THE PROFESSIONAL TUTOR'S ROLE

I have said very little about the role of the professional tutor in the overall delivery of ITT; it will clearly vary according to his or her position within the school. HEIs are playing a major part in the development of this role through the expectations they are putting forward as laid down in their partnership contracts with schools. Generally speaking, the professional tutor has overall responsibility for the experience of all ITT students in school, ensuring that the programmes of study are followed, liaising closely with the partner institutions, leading the team of mentors, facilitating seminars for students and overseeing the production of course work assignments as required. The professional tutor also has the responsibility for keeping himself or herself fully informed about the progress of individual ITT students, counselling where necessary and collating reports.

To successfully carry out a professional tutor's role takes more than this, however. It is up to the professional tutor to take the lead and create a positive climate for this new and major area of development within our schools. The professional tutor must:

- have the ideas and the credibility to set up a forum for the discussion of those ideas and the status to put them into practice;
- encourage colleagues in all areas of the school to contribute their expertise and facilitate the development of their interests and skills;
- ensure the quality control of not only what is being offered to student teachers but of what is being delivered in the classroom.

To have any chance at all of tackling at least some of these tasks with success, the professional tutor also needs the constant and constructive support of a committed team of mentors. I have been most fortunate in working with such a team.

BENEFITS OF ITT WORK

We have enjoyed our new partnerships with higher education and the new opportunities which are now being presented to teachers in schools for training the next generation of secondary subject teachers. Some of us have been actively involved in the steering groups initiated by our partner institutions, at both subject and general management level, to explore ways to monitor, further develop and improve upon current practice in ITT. In one instance we have drawn up joint programmes with the institution to ensure that the training which takes place in the school dovetails with that in the HEI.

The links that have been built up with university and college tutors are highly valued but the last word has to be about whether, through our school-wide commitment to our ITT role, we are managing to improve the quality of what is being delivered to our pupils in the classroom. Our experiences so far suggest that this is indeed the case, and this is also borne out by overall studies of similar schemes to ours (McIntyre, Hagger and Burn, 1994, pp. 96–115).

Pupils have benefited from the freshness and additional expertise being brought into their learning by the involvement of ITT students in delivering the curriculum. Supervising teachers, conscious of the importance of themselves as professional role models to ITT trainees, have had to examine their own practices; they have also had to consider the best ways of managing different practices such as collaborative teaching. In terms of staff development it has been a delight to see teachers blossom with a new-found confidence and buoyancy as a result of their work with students, as mentors or as classroom teachers. (Again see McIntyre, Hagger and Burn, 1994, for further examples of this, in other schools as well.)

The effect of involvement in the ITT partnership on teacher morale has been very positive. The school as a whole has also felt the benefits of having ITT students on site for a large proportion of the year. Students who spend a substantial portion of their time in one school become much more committed to it. They participate in extra-curricular activities, attend parents' consultation evenings, accompany school trips, run clubs and become involved in the pastoral curriculum. When the opportunities have been there a number of 'our' trainees have applied for employment with us on completion of their training – and have been successful in their applications. The increased expertise of these newly qualified teachers has meant that we are now having to re-think our programme of induction and training of beginning teachers: those just embarking on their teaching careers, having successfully passed through a period of ITT. We now have a team of mentors in the school with responsibility for the successful induction of beginning teachers, and they are meeting regularly to develop their induction programmes and ways of monitoring overall progress, but that is another story . . .

My thanks to the mentors of South Coast Community School for all their commitment and support in the writing of this chapter.

10

INTELLECTUAL CHALLENGES FOR PARTNERSHIP

Pat Drake and Lisa Dart

Since the publication of CATE criteria for secondary and primary initial teacher training (DFE, 1992 and 1993) there has been a flurry of interest in the respective activities of school and university partners in the training process. Through collaboration between schools and higher education institutions, administrative, financial and practical arrangements are made. The complexity of these tasks is highlighted by the tension with which all those involved in the process are familiar. Typically, institutions negotiate with each other through partnership committees for an appropriate degree of involvement which is commensurate with an acceptable funding level. The more schools in partnership with an institution, the more individual programmes within each school must then be incorporated into coherent provision across the partnership. A well documented difficulty is the tension for schools between fulfilling their obligations to their pupils and participating in the training process (UCET, 1994). For many, this contributory factor prevents them from developing school-centred schemes for themselves.

Usually secondary schools agree to provide trainee teachers with a subject 'mentor' and some designated time for 'mentoring' regularly during the school placement. Transfer of funding from the HEI may be contingent on this provision. Opportunity for intellectual engagement with teaching is now afforded through the mentor-trainee meeting, which provides the interface between the novice and the experienced teacher.

Competence of newly qualified teachers is assessed in the following areas:

- subject knowledge
- subject application
- classroom management
- assessment and recording of pupils' progress
- further professional development

© 1995 Pat Drake and Lisa Dart

and is required of novice secondary school teachers by the time they qualify. The large proportion of time (currently twenty-four weeks out of a possible thirty-six on secondary courses) that novices spend in school clearly increases the responsibility of the mentor for ensuring development in these areas. The challenge facing partners is how to sustain intellectual reflection on the part of the trainee as competence develops, in the teeth of a tendency for the hugely complex and tension-ridden administrative requirements of maintaining partnership to overwhelm intellectual issues. Of particular interest, because of increased time in school, are the areas of subject knowledge and subject application.

The hour per week timetabled for trainees and mentors in the Sussex secondary PGCE scheme has enabled a research project[1] to focus on how that hour is used. In particular we have been concerned with how trainee teachers and mentors deal with issues pertaining specifically to the subjects of secondary school English and mathematics. We assumed that this timetabled mentor time is significant in the induction of the trainee teacher into the subject culture. The research has revealed that mentors do construct and express critical perspectives on teaching and learning school mathematics and English in working with trainee teachers. What appears to be problematic is a tendency for trainee teachers not to engage with the critical perspectives offered to them in school; this may be for a variety of reasons which we discuss later. Also, perhaps through lack of opportunity, there is limited acknowledgement by mentors that their own beliefs implicitly generate philosophies of teaching and learning in their subject. This matters because it is likely that these beliefs will influence mentors' judgements about competence.

Furlong *et al.* (1988) identify four levels of training in *Initial Teacher Training and the Role of the School*:

- direct practice
- indirect practice
- practical principles
- and disciplinary theory.

In the years since this study was written partnerships have evolved so that any hierarchy implied by the use of the term 'level' is challenged. Nevertheless it is true that in a partnership model of training, direct practice (i.e. the development of knowledge, skills and understanding through immediate first-hand experience) is afforded considerable importance, with trainee teachers being implicitly trained to act according to practical principles exemplified in the pragmatics of everyday classroom practice. One contribution of university staff, suggest Furlong and his colleagues, is to make trainee teachers explicitly face the unconscious practical principles on which they operate. This requires dedicated time which, at the university, becomes more difficult to find when a large number of requirements have to be met; and small group teaching, which is expensive to provide. Less time at the university, bluntly, allows less time for reflection on practice to happen there.

In anticipating the shift towards school-based teacher education, commentators have identified in more detail aspects of the process expedited by school tutors. Wiliam (1994) points out that tuition on school-based schemes is costly and so it is of fundamental importance that the interaction between trainee and mentor is effective. Generic, i.e. similar across different subjects, mentoring practices through which practical teacher development is facilitated have been identified by, amongst others, Wilkin (1992), Dart and Drake (1993) and McIntyre *et al.* (1993). So, for example, the mentor will often be responsible for co-ordinating the passing on of feedback to the trainee teacher from other teachers within the subject department. There is the potential for unwittingly inhibiting trainee progress, too, within these general activities. For instance, using the above example we report elsewhere (Dart and Drake, 1993) how trainees may perceive themselves to be on the receiving end of contradictory advice at best, or a 'personality clash' at worst should critical feedback from one teacher not be verbally substantiated by another.

In the field of subject knowledge the evidence is less clear. Ruthven (1993) suggests that three forms of professional knowledge are drawn upon by expert teachers: tacit expertise, with which skilful teachers make sense of and act upon in teaching situations; pragmatic wisdom, by which is meant the generally accepted perceptions of good practice which permeate the teaching of a subject; and grounded science, indicating a basis for action which takes account of research into the teaching and learning of, in the context of Ruthven's work, school mathematics. He suggests that expert teachers manage a repertoire of teaching activities implicitly drawing upon and relating their knowledge in these domains. Furthermore, he argues that unless a novice or trainee teacher has access to these forms of knowledge, he or she will be unable to make sense of the classroom behaviour exhibited by experienced teachers. This point is supported by Cooper (1990) who, in a study of mathematics PGCE students, revealed specific anxieties in the area of investigational mathematics.[2] These anxieties are consistent with the inexperience that novice teachers typically have of doing investigational work at school themselves, and the inaccessibility of the practice of their experienced colleagues in school.

Experienced teachers, on the other hand, in making judgements about the progress of trainees, and deeming them to be competent, will bring to bear their own beliefs and value systems about the teaching of the subject (Crosson and Shiu, 1994). Sanders (1994), in her examination of mentors' personal views of mathematics teaching, draws to our attention the wide ranging philosophies held by mathematics teachers about mathematics itself. She reminds us of our own experience as pupils on the receiving end of these philosophies, and how our perceptions of the subject are shaped by teachers who, for example insisted on following the rules, or as a contrast, encouraged us to find our own errors and to thereby develop our own understanding. In an earlier phase of our own study (Drake and Dart, 1994) 'English mentors expressed beliefs which were, for some, formulated in terms of a traditional approach to literature; an awareness of the need to teach the National Curriculum and to tackle issues arising from basic skills of punctuation, spelling and grammar which was often combined with a political sensitivity to the conservative nature of addressing these skills; a knowledge about the impact of theories such as post-structuralism and their potential for offering different exploration of text; and also the skills of being organised, a manager, and an effective member of a team.' In other words, a range of differing perspectives prevails in English too.

The potential for sinking into a quagmire of difficulty and delusion faces mentors charged with responsibility for the assessment of trainee teachers and designating them as 'competent' according to the specified CATE criteria. In the first place, by stating that a teacher is competent by implication there exists the possibility of being 'not competent'. In either case the trainee teacher is perfectly justified in demanding to know the criteria by which he or she is judged, what the evidence base is for such judgements, whether the judgements would have been different in a different context and if so why that context was not provided, and so on.

Now this is a problem not just in training teachers, but for the whole teaching profession. Eraut (1994) discusses how the competence model in initial teacher education in England and Wales differs from that of other professions. For teaching, unlike other occupations, does not have a long post-qualification graduation. Newly qualified teachers are expected to be competent, and to practise with very little support immediately they have undergone the initial training period. This requires an assumption to be made, namely that competence in the training context (typically two schools only, relatively close to each other geographically) implies competence in any other context and location. Eraut develops a useful argument describing a concept he calls 'capability', a parameter for supplementing the assessment of the professional aptitude across a number of professions, including teaching. He writes:

> We found it useful to discuss evidence of professional competence under two main headings: performance and capability. Performance evidence does of course provide evidence of capability; but the term 'capability evidence' is used to refer to evidence not directly derived from normal performance on the job. Sometimes the purpose of capability evidence was to supplement performance evidence, sometimes it was to ascertain the candidate's potential to perform in the future.
>
> (Michael Eraut, 1994, p. 200)

Thus the capability evidence for newly qualified teachers consists of evidence, usually documentary, demonstrating that the trainee, as well as demonstrating successful practice in school, is also likely to be able to transfer their professional skill to a different school context.

However, as we have argued elsewhere (op. cit.) variation between subjects is likely to result in different interpretations and applications of the criteria in subject knowledge and subject application. It is likely, too, that the different attitudes held by teachers within a subject will affect their perception of trainees' participation and performance. There is a danger, which is likely to affect particularly those trainees who are perceived to be weak, that judgements of competence may be made on the basis not of performance or capability evidence, but on a holistic assessment of potential. Then implicit and inarticulated beliefs may be drawn upon and brought to bear. Thus in the light of the quest for competence it is important for trainees to draw upon any articulation by their school tutors of their subject beliefs, philosophy and pedagogic professional knowledge.

In this chapter we draw upon tape recorded sessions between seven mentor-trainee pairs, three in English and four in mathematics. At the time of these sessions, in March 1994, the trainees were fourteen, fifteen or sixteen weeks in to their first school experience, and had begun a block of six weeks in school full-time. Each mentor had already been interviewed as part of the project, and had read and commented on a transcript of the interview. All had agreed with their trainee to continue their involvement by recording on a blank tape sent through the post to them at school one of the timetabled mentor sessions. The data is rich, and interpretable on several dimensions. For example, similarities and differences between English and mathematics practices are described elsewhere (Drake and Dart, 1994), as are issues related to constructing subject knowledge (Dart and Drake, 1995). The focus here is on instances where the taped sessions provide examples of explicit issues which we believe may typify aspects of the struggle by trainee teachers to become recognised as competent to teach their subject. These issues offer some challenges for the development of new teachers in becoming aware of how the intellectual demands of teaching a subject integrate with practical classroom concerns. In particular, we identify features of interaction between mentors and trainees which it would seem to be appropriate to address explicitly within the training process. The chapter concludes by drawing out implications of the research findings for initial teacher education in general and the training of mentors in particular, by pointing to the relevance and application of specific disciplinary characteristics in the closely interrelated processes of mentoring and mentorship training.[3]

AVOIDING THE ISSUE

A feature of the interviews was the degree of success with which trainees were able to turn the conversation either towards or away from specific topics, themes or questions introduced by the mentor. Of course the existence of the tape recorder in the mentor-trainee sessions did have an effect on the conduct of the interview. Participants admitted to feeling a need to keep the conversation going, for example, when more naturally it might have stopped. Trainees are vulnerable to criticism from their mentors anyway. Under normal circumstances any comments made would have been private and finished with at the end of the meeting, not pored over by researchers (who were also trainees' university tutors) searching for evidence. Perhaps it is not then surprising to note that on the tapes there seemed to be a tendency on the part of trainees to sidestep challenges. For instance, a mathematics mentor, picking up a suggestion from the trainee that a lower-ability year-10 group might plan a day trip, develops some thoughts on the question of how in real life the direct application of mathematics is tempered by other concerns:

> M: You know I save money by going by bus, but I get there two hours late. So those sorts of decisions are quite often involved when you're thinking about the kind of problems people solve in their day-to-day life. It brings home a different flavour to the text book approach of 'here's ten questions and normally there's a right answer'. There isn't a right answer to questions like that . . . that's quite good.
>
> T: I think there's lots of different things for them to look at, a lot of decisions to make, should they bring their lunch, will they want to buy a souvenir. I'm sure they will come up with many more ideas than I have right now.
>
> (Mathematics: male mentor and female trainee)

The trainee returns the discussion back to practical concerns, e.g. lunch, and then terminates it by saying that she has no more ideas, so arguably disregarding the invitation from the mentor to engage intellectually with the idea that there may be a useful contrast to be made between school mathematics and mathematical decision-making in real life.

One trainee, an English student, made a direct appeal to the tape recorder:

> M: How are you going to explain it to Year 11, as you go on, the purpose of what they're doing? While they're doing it?
>
> T: This is a familiar question that I get in my mentor sessions. Why are they doing it? I don't know, I often get stumped by this question I have to say.
>
> (English: male mentor and male trainee)

Here too the trainee (possibly the mentor too) avoided the opportunity to engage intellectually with a critical appraisal of teaching English.

Our focus on specific subject issues led us to anticipate difficulty for trainees in some areas, for instance working investigationally in mathematics, or teaching grammar in English. Indeed these were apparent issues for trainees, but in the context of the mentor-trainee session the difficulty of receiving criticism was more apparent when (in the mentor's view) a pedagogic approach was not sufficiently justified.

M: Did you draw any distinctions for them between the use of standard and non-standard English?

T: Yeah, yeah we've done that before. Once I made explicit what I was looking for, I was giving them freedom, they seemed to enjoy it more. And I thought that they can get from Shakespeare's language to their own language, well they bypass, they have to go through standard English anyway to get there.

M: Not necessarily. They could leave out standard English depending on their own grasp of it.

T: But within their own thought processes surely they have to translate a couple of times to get to where they are?

M: Again not necessarily . . .

T: To me it seemed that that was the way they were doing it . . . And that was the end of the lesson and I didn't think it worth continuing today so I've given them a worksheet to finish it off.

(English: male mentor and male trainee)

The mentor attempts to question critically the intellectual basis for the pedagogy of the trainee but again is rebuffed.

The length of time that trainees had been in school may be significant in the above examples, in so far as trainees were by this time expecting to 'manage' classes on their own. It may be that classroom management is paramount to the extent that other considerations are just not taken on board at that stage of training. (See, for example, Fuller, 1970, for a model of practitioner development.) University staff working on non-school based PGCEs have, informally at least, always had to acknowledge difficulty in persuading trainee teachers to consider and experiment with a range of alternative pedagogy. Resistance was often expressed in terms of criticism that university tutors did not have a realistic enough working knowledge of the school context. Often the school supervisor was supportive of the trainee's position, recognising the need for the trainee to comply with school norms of classroom management in order to pass the teaching practice. The evidence in this data drawn from a school-based scheme suggests, alarmingly, that the same, or similar, phenomenon of resistance to critical reflection on pedagogy may prevail between school mentor and trainee. It is important that this issue be made explicit and addressed directly by school and university staff.

What these extracts from the transcripts do not convey is the mutual regard (or otherwise) between mentor and trainee. However, we suspect that a contributing factor in breakdowns of the relationship may be when the trainee is consistently unable to make sense of the intellectual perspective of the mentor, let alone agree or disagree with it.

LEARNING OF SUBJECT MATTER ON THE HOOF

It is an expectation on the part of teachers that one deepens subject under-standing through teaching. Now it is also required that teachers learn and relearn new topics as the curriculum changes. In trying to identify areas in which mentors play a part in prompting the acquisition and development of subject knowledge, we asked them to consider the possibility of a 'gap' between the subject knowledge with which the trainee teacher arrived on the PGCE and that which is required to teach mathematics or English in school. We also analysed the recordings of the mentor-trainee sessions for references or allusions to lack of subject knowledge or skill. Among the issues which emerged were differences between the subject at school level when the trainee is likely to have studied it and what is in the school subject now, and differences between the subject as studied at university and what is appropriate for school. The evidence from the mathematics participants is generally framed in terms of changes in school mathematics over time. There were few references to university mathematics. Specific deficiencies in content knowledge are not seen on the part of mentors as problematic, as it is acknowledged that all teachers of mathematics have often had to learn and relearn new content areas. There are several examples: for instance one mathematics mentor pointed out that, because of the introduction of handling data into the school mathematics curriculum, 'there will be people teaching things like standard deviation who have never taught it in their lives, and may have done it if they're lucky in their degree. The chances are they didn't, so they're having to relearn. It's not just unique to students' (Mathematics: male mentor, head of department).

Our data revealed that trainees are expected to do a great deal of consolidation of new content themselves, in both mathematics and English.

M: Try to get them to get print-outs of their graphs so they can put them in their books.

T: Okay, yes. Graphs, print-outs, I'll have to work out how to do that.

M: Yep.

Sometimes the realisation that there may be completely new aspects of the subject comes as quite a shock:

T: Differences are something I've only come across through my own foster daughter. Despite having a maths degree I never did differences, ever.

M: Really?

T: And I actually discovered through something she did at A-level – I didn't realise that there are difference equations that follow the same rules as differential equations.

M: That's right.

T: And I thought 'wow, why haven't I? I've got a good mathematics degree and no one has ever shown me!'

(Mathematics: male mentor and male trainee)

The assumption that people can 'mug up' as they go along does raise some concerns. Firstly it takes time, which currently is not allowed for. Secondly the trainee may actually be unaware that he or she has a gap in a particular area. Thirdly the mentor may want to monitor trainees' progress in updating their subject knowledge, and this may be difficult to do reactively. This next extract provides an example of a mentor making sure that a mathematics trainee is fully briefed on the mathematical ideas underlying an activity. Not everyone is able to be as tactful as the mentor in the extract, where the careful use of the word 'student' prevents the trainee from explicitly revealing any ignorance of their own.

M: Yep. And what about prime numbers? How did the students go about finding whether the number was prime or not?

T: If it had any factors other than itself and one.

M: Right, and how did they do that?

T: They would look at the number and they would say what goes into this number? And when they came up with nothing except that number and one they would move on to the next number.

M: So if I gave one of those students a number, say 319, what do you think they would do?

T: Well, first they would look at the unit's digit and see that it's a nine, an odd number, so two won't go into it.

M: Right.

T: Then they'd go up. Well let's see, does three go into it, does four go into it, does five go into it?

M: Where would they stop?

T: Where would they stop? I don't know.

M: Well, the point I'm driving at is that it's quite interesting that if you give students a thing like that and a calculator . . . the question invariably comes up where do they stop?

T: I'd assume they'd stop half way.

M: Well a lot of students think it's half way, but in actual fact you only need to go up to the square root of the number because after that any number will pair off. Do you see what I mean?

T: Right, yeah . . .

(Mathematics: male mentor and female trainee)

English mentors tended to contrast university English studies with the subject at school, both in terms of content, and style of teaching and learning. As one mentor put it, English degrees tend to be 'literature-based, and so much of the national curriculum is not literature-based, it includes drama, it includes English language'. Even when literature is studied at school it is unlikely to be 'the sort of literature that you study at university'. One mentor reflected that she had, on a rare occasion when the content was similar, neglected to clarify with the trainee her view that a different approach would be required:

> She put a Shakespeare sonnet in front of them. I was sitting in the cupboard listening to this, and she launched straight in to work on the structure of the sonnet, rhyme scheme with syllables, two lines, all different stresses in the line. It never occurred to me that she would look at the structure rather than the meaning. And of course you've got to look at the meaning of a poem first, especially something like a Shakespearean sonnet which as far as they were concerned had just landed from the moon.
>
> (English: female mentor, head of department)

Teachers of English recognise that differences in the subject now, especially skills with language grammar and syntax, may be new for trainee teachers. The following English mentor questions the two trainees in her department about their technical skills:

M: Would you know if a child didn't know how to pronounce new words, would you know how to teach them?

T1: Personally, if they were having such problems I would refer them for special needs help.

T2: Practically I don't know how I would go about it, in the classroom, I would probably do the wrong thing and do it for them.

M: So some sort of knowledge on your part would help.

T1: Yes. I came across a word the other day that I'd never seen before, 'assuage', and it was like being 14 again.

M: Are there other subject-specific skills? Is it your duty to be a good speller? (laughter)

T1: No, I think it's your duty to know what your limitations are so if you know you have a failing in spelling you should have a dictionary.

(English: female mentor, T1 male, T2 female)

English mentors take different positions with respect to this issue. Contrast the mentor who says that she herself attended 'a grammar school which took the word grammar rather literally' with another who states that 'a number of people find it difficult to know when to use speech marks and full stops even when they're writing on the board'. The first mentor declares that 'we do have students (teachers) who don't understand it but it's hardly of prime importance, you can mug up on it, it's sensitivity to language that counts'. The second mentor disagrees: 'I don't think it's a very good example to pupils if teachers are making spelling mistakes on the board'.

The range and variety of subject issues discussed during the mentor-trainee sessions is obviously related to the individuals concerned, and their needs as they perceive them. Talking through content issues, especially in mathematics, may serve also to update the knowledge of the mentor as well as that of the trainee. In particular, trainees' computing skills are valued. Indeed, one of the reasons mentors give for enjoying their work with trainee teachers is that it 'brings in new ideas'. Mentors in our study were forgiving towards trainees' apparent gaps, and recognised through their experience that part of the training process involves addressing subject knowledge.

DIFFERENT DISCOURSE

Teaching and learning a subject requires judgement on the part of the teacher about appropriate contexts for the classroom activity. The contexts chosen will depend upon assumptions by the teachers as to their suitability and efficacy. Sensitive issues may need to be considered here. For example, some years ago the whole question of the political neutrality of school mathematics was called into question by the publication of what came to be known as the 'anti-racist banana'. This depicted a diagram of a banana divided into sections according to the proportion of the 10p selling price which went to the grower, the picker, the exporter/importer, the greengrocer etc. The then Prime Minister, Margaret Thatcher, was reported to denounce 'anti-racist mathematics, whatever that might be'.[4] The following extract may be quite typical of situations where the mentor and trainee may hold very different perspectives, may operate in different discourses, and may not, in fact, establish the kind of mutuality of ideas which leads to a successful working relationship. The trainee, who was himself Asian British, attempts to engage his mentor in a discussion of how to introduce a consideration of racism into the English classroom:

T: I found an article from the essential articles, an Asian woman talking about what it is to be Asian British, and all she's really talking about is what it is to be herself, views on race from quite a personal stance. I think that is what A [another teacher whose class T teaches] wants me to do, that sort of thing. It's culled from I think *Marxism Today*.

M: Have you seen *A Sikh by Night*?

T: No.

M: Let me just get that.

T: Yeah. No, this is good, this is similar to the article that I've got, where this girl was saying how she'd denied her Asian side, she had an Asian name and she kind of Anglicised it.

M: Anyway look at that one and see what you think. There is as I said a whole set of them if you need them.

T: And as they've been through it with A they should have their own views. And I told them the front page of their story is going to be a racial attack, and they can take it . . . (tape ends).

In apparently attempting to help the trainee by suggesting *A Sikh by Night* the mentor detaches from the approach being proposed by the trainee. The rest of the extract can be interpreted as both individuals continuing along distinctly separate lines of thought. There are a number of instances in the tapes where this happens. Most of them form conversations too long to include here, but they are typified by the mentor attempting to persuade the trainee to use a pedagogic approach which the trainee, for whatever reason, resists (Dart and Drake, in preparation). In this category we find, for example, oblique discussions about using computers, or investigational mathematics. It is this category which is particularly difficult to address in the training session, as neither trainee nor mentor may be aware that the other is working from a different set of principles or beliefs. For instance, in one session a mathematics mentor and trainee are discussing a computer lesson with year 8. The mentor is critical of the lesson and tries to draw the attention of the trainee to distinguish between the understanding and knowledge required by the pupils to *begin* the task set by the trainee (to draw a circle on the computer screen), and the skills and knowledge acquired by the pupils in *completing* the task. The trainee does not engage with this line of argument, instead reflecting on his choice of activity (using the computers) and how intrinsically motivating it was:

> I find it very difficult to judge their motivation. That's the thing. I would have assumed that putting them in front of the computers is a fantastic thing to do in the first place, because it would have been when I was at school basically. And I wasn't too concerned if they weren't doing exactly as I'd asked them, as long as they were trying commands and working.
>
> (Mathematics: male trainee)

CONCLUSION

The circumstances we have described prevail in a profession whose expectations and description of competence can lead to considerable variations in interpretation. This is not only because of the differing, and hitherto undebated, perspectives brought to bear by mentors about their subject. It is important to recognise that different interpretations also result from unclear expectations of what it is that new teachers are realistically expected actually to be able to do. Competence statements (without an accompanying range of contexts from which evidence can be collected) describe good practice, or professional norms, for experienced practitioners. They serve as public descriptions of what the profession actually does. It is very clear, therefore, that mentors are acting as gatekeepers to the profession, and that declarations of competence of trainees in themselves testify to there being appropriate overall professional standards.

In summary our data reveal that the discourse between trainee and mentor serves a rich and extensive set of purposes. In particular, we have argued that three areas which come under the headings of 'avoiding the issue', 'learning on the hoof' and 'different discourse' are distinctive and recognisable in the context of training mathematics and English teachers. Teachers of different school subjects may well be able to add to the list. Whilst our evidence is drawn from the discourse between mentor and trainee, the implications extend beyond the boundaries of that relationship. As teacher training becomes embedded in schools, school and university tutors together are drawn more towards joint reflection on their practices as teachers and teacher educators. Activities are being reassigned, roles are becoming recast. No longer is it appropriate to think simply of dividing the list of competences to 'cover' between school and HEI. Mutuality of purpose exists and it is increasingly difficult, even if it were to be desirable, to differentiate functionally between teaching (in school), teacher education and training trainers. Clearly, though, there is scope for complementary activity in the particular areas of subject knowledge and subject application. It is through rigorous examination by school and university tutors together of the intellectual practices of teaching that development can occur most fruitfully, and it is our belief that it is in this direction that teacher educators should turn.

ACKNOWLEDGEMENTS

We are indebted to the Paul Hamlyn Foundation and Esmée Fairbairn Charitable Trust for supporting our research, and to Tony Becher without whose help and encouragement this would not have been written. We are grateful too to Michael Eraut whose precise comments focused the discussion of competence much more sharply.

We would also like to thank particularly the teachers involved in the project: Chris Anderson, Alison Browning, Krys Buleska, Adrian Burnett, Elaine Comisky, Rowland Darby, Teresa Dickens, Ella Dzelzainis, John Heaton, Adrian Hinckley, Wayne Jones, Ken Leonard, Elizabeth Lockwood, Deidra McCloughlin, Uday Patel, Keith Perera, Eddie Slater, Sarah Smith and Gill

Weinrib. We are most grateful to them for trusting us with their thoughts and words, and hope that we have represented them with integrity.

NOTES

1. The Esmée Fairbairn Research project 1993–95 was a collaborative venture between the Universities of Oxford, Manchester Metropolitan, Swansea, Keele, Leicester and Sussex.

2. Mathematics in the National Curriculum having, at the time of writing, undergone another reconstitution includes five attainment targets at Key Stages 3 and 4: Using and Applying Mathematics; Number; Algebra; Shape, Space and Measure; Handling Data. Using and Applying Mathematics is usually interpreted to mean investigational work.

3. In all the extracts from interviews, T is trainee and M is mentor.

4. This exchange, in 1983, coincided with the publication of an A-level mathematics examination question about a bomb dropping and sinking a ship, and was in the same year as the sinking by HM forces of a ship, the *Belgrano*, during the Falklands War.

SECTION FOUR

Looking Ahead: The Way Forward for Partnership

11

IMPLICATIONS FOR SCHOOLS OF RECENT CHANGES IN INITIAL TEACHER EDUCATION: A NATIONAL UNION OF TEACHERS VIEWPOINT

Kate Ring

In this chapter the effects of moves towards more school-centred schemes of ITE will be discussed, with particular consideration of the impact which such schemes are having, and are likely to have, on the professional lives of the teaching staff involved and on the schools in which they take place.

The need to retain a role for HEIs is stressed, and basic principles advocated by the National Union of Teachers (NUT) for the successful development, organisation and operation of partnership schemes of school-based ITE are described. The chapter also deals with the central role and impact of the Teacher Training Agency (TTA) and examines OFSTED's approach to the changing situation.

Given satisfactory levels of resourcing and training, and proper acknowledgement of the contribution to be made by all those involved, from both schools and HEIs – as well as the ITE students themselves – there is certainly no reason why school-based partnership schemes of ITE across all phases should not prove to be a successful means of providing high standards of professional training for a new generation of teachers, while providing real benefits to all areas of the education system involved.

Two years ago, in 1993, the National Union of Teachers held a national one-day conference on initial teacher education in London. The theme was *Teacher Education Today and Tomorrow* and the aim was to set the agenda for Union policy, in the face of government changes which, it was acknowledged, could have both far-reaching and potentially catastrophic consequences.

Two years on it is reassuring that no catastrophes have come about. In part this must be due to the commitment of higher education institutions to maintaining and developing workable relationships with schools. Credit too must be given to the great majority of schools themselves, who have not pulled out of ITE but whose commitment to involvement remains, for the time being, intact. What is certain, however, is that the next two years will be even more significant, in the extent to which the delicate relationships between HEIs and schools evolve and to which the Teacher Training Agency, in presiding over and encouraging partnership arrangements, does so in a professional and even-handed manner.

Until 1992 government policy on initial teacher education had yet to surface from the depths of controversy in which policy change in other areas had been submerged, namely the National Curriculum and assessment arrangements, the privatisation of the school inspectorate and the break-up of local education authorities. Kenneth Clarke's announcement made in a speech to the North of England Conference in January of that year, that 80 per cent of secondary initial teacher education should take place in schools, was one of the statements that caused ITE to break the surface as the next issue for government 'reform'.

The shift to school-based training was greeted with considerable irony by teachers, reflecting on the criticisms levelled at them by the Secretary of State who was now proposing that they take greater responsibility for training future members of the profession. The NUT was not alone in identifying the main driving forces behind the government's policy changes as being the same as those underlying all reform in education since 1988.

The determination to strictly inhibit public expenditure and to simultaneously impose the market forces 'solution' on the education service was being brought to bear on this, as yet, relatively unscathed sector. True, the government had recently announced the first round of pilot school-centred ITE schemes (SCITTs). At the time of the 1993 NUT Conference rumours abounded about the likely content and implications of the long delayed proposals for the reform of primary ITE. In spite of the fact that Circular 9/92 did not, in the end, push the responsibility for training wholly into schools, the practicalities of partnership were, nevertheless, testing the government's assumption that equal partnerships would be guaranteed, simply through a transfer of resources from HEIs into schools.

Perhaps it was Education Secretary John Patten's mismanagement of the proposal for a one-year training route for nursery and Key Stage 1 teachers which awakened the teaching profession as a whole to the likely implications of the government's changes. Certainly, Qualified Teacher Status was suddenly the phrase on many people's lips. John Patten's bungled attempt to introduce the one-year route resulted in a united backlash from teachers, parents and governors against the proposal, which it would have been difficult to organise, had there not been help from the Secretary of State.

The dangers of a disunited response to changes in ITE were, nonetheless, only too obvious. Indeed, it is worth reflecting on the salutary warning given to the NUT conference in 1993 by Michael Barber:

A likely response of the education sector, if it remains true to form, will not be a united rejection but an undignified squabble between participants over excessively limited resources: musical chairs with many participants and too few chairs. If this is the profession's response, then it would be the equivalent of the profession contributing to its own destruction; not so much turkeys voting for Christmas, as turkeys squabbling so much they do not even notice it coming.

(Barber, 1993)

Another commentator, this time Stuart Maclure, characterised the dilemma facing those in the process of imposing change on initial teacher education, in this case the then Secretary of State:

He knows he cannot take the professional training of teachers out of higher education in one fell swoop. So he is like a man looking for ways of crossing a swiftly flowing river – he first has to lay down stepping stones. Flattering teachers (and offering financial inducements to take over the training function) is a first step in creating a viable alternative to the present training mechanism.

(Maclure, 1993)

Two years on it does not look as though that strategy has succeeded. Although, at the time of writing, no independent evaluation of the success or otherwise of school-centred ITT schemes is available, what is clear is that both schools themselves and the newly established Teacher Training Agency are proceeding with caution in the extent to which they embrace or encourage those arrangements.

For the profession as a whole this caution has two significant implications. The first is that HEIs and schools must seize the opportunity to discuss openly the obstacles to be overcome before the division of roles and responsibilities between them, in relation to the initial education of teachers, can be approached. Secondly, and more importantly, there is time for us all to learn from the examples of successful partnerships which are currently operating and to ask questions about the reasons for their success.

In an attempt to facilitate successful negotiation on involvement in partnerships for its members, the NUT in the summer of 1994 finally published its advice to schools. That advice has been disseminated widely, with copies being sent to every HEI in England and Wales, as well as to every school. The premise of the Union's advice, along with the need to protect teachers' interests, is that high quality ITE and the maintenance of all-graduate entry to teaching are vital for the education service. Initial teacher education must focus on developing teachers as professional practitioners. There is, therefore, in the Union's view, no debate about the need for a significant amount of ITE to be based in schools. Neither, unfortunately, is there any debate about the fact that schools have not always been treated as equal partners in the training process. For new partnerships to work this has to change.

For the time being, then, the debate has shifted slightly since Rosalind

Goodyear and Vivienne Little described the history of the education and training of teachers in England and Wales (Goodyear and Little, 1993). The polarised debate about where, how and why teachers should be trained has, for the moment anyway, given way to discussion about who has responsibility for training and how, therefore, they should be prepared and supported to undertake that role. This is not to dismiss the important debate about why we train teachers and the methods we employ. Rather, it is to give that debate an important new emphasis. It is in discussions about responsibilities and accountabilities in relation to training teachers that concrete solutions to the very real questions about what sort of teachers we are preparing for the future are likely to be found.

Turning now to the detail of the Union's advice, it is important to preface it with some acknowledged facts. Schools benefit to a significant degree and in a number of ways from involvement in ITE. A good ITE student is an asset in as much as a weak student can be a liability to a school. A number of good students in one school can contribute significantly towards enhancing the quality of learning for pupils.

Resources made available to schools and individual teachers in respect of training can mean that considerable opportunities for professional development are opened up, as a direct result of involvement in ITE. Schools, teachers, and often pupils, gain a fresh and sometimes expert perspective on a subject or subjects from good students who bring with them enthusiasm and in-depth knowledge of their main area of study. OFSTED has reported on the positive effects in small primary schools of students bringing with them to their teaching placements up-to-date, detailed knowledge of a subject with which established teachers are less confident (OFSTED, 1993).

From the point of view of the ITE student, school experience means increased opportunities to meet, talk with, think and feel alongside experienced teachers. An understanding of schools as organisations, and of their links with the surrounding community and above all an appreciation of that vital relationship between school, parents and children, can only really develop for students while they are on placement in school. Crucially, however, the sifting of gathered experiences and the assigning of understanding to those experiences require the reflective context available specifically in the HEI itself. Conversely, inherited experience in a school can easily turn into narrowly focused parochialism. A school can provide a group of richly experienced, professional, humorous and thoughtful teachers to welcome a student or, as we all know, it can present a frazzled, disillusioned and unwelcoming setting for a teaching practice.

Teachers' workloads are currently at record levels. To take for granted, therefore, the enthusiasm and commitment of teachers to participation in ITE would be a great mistake. An acknowledgement of teachers' workloads must be built into any new and on-going partnership discussions.

Resourcing for school-based training of student teachers is an area with considerable potential for problems. The destination of resources allocated to schools in respect of their ITE responsibilities is not always known. Certainly, resources coming into a school do not always seem to benefit directly either the teachers involved in training or the students themselves. This is one aspect of the new arrangements which must be nailed down if partnerships are to succeed. There is little point in claiming that resources are inadequate if it is not actually known how much a school is receiving in respect of taking on the responsibility of a student in the first place. Negotiation about resources needs to involve far more people than is currently the case and must be based on clearly agreed criteria.

As a teacher trade union the NUT must provide constructive advice to members which will protect them in relation to workload and involvement in ITE. As well as partnership arrangements, some of our members will be involved in the pilot school-centred schemes. Substantial numbers of members are also involved in the Open University distance-learning PGCE. Union advice, by definition, must cover a wide range of eventualities.

That advice is based on sound policy principles which are:

- That all courses must include a significant HEI course of study.
- That all courses must lead to a qualification which is acceptable for the purposes of validation by an HEI.
- That all courses must provide student teachers with significant experience in a variety of schools and a guarantee that there will be an opportunity to change school if a placement does not work out.
- That all courses should have mentors or teacher tutors with sufficient and appropriate training, preparation and resources, including cover and a reduced timetable, to allow them to fulfil responsibilities without additional workload.
- That all courses should have guaranteed funding over time and sufficient resourcing to ensure that a school's primary responsibility, teaching pupils, is not put at risk.
- That all courses should exclude students from the staffing complement of the school in which they are placed.
- That all partnership arrangements, including those arrived at through SCITTs, must be the subject of detailed consultation with the school, its staff, governors, parents and, where appropriate, pupils and the HEI concerned.

(NUT, 1994)

Certainly, neither the TTA nor any other body should be in the business of promoting involvement in wholly school-centred schemes at the expense of appropriately constituted partnerships properly negotiated between schools and HEIs. The research and reflective approaches of HEIs complement the practical skills of teaching, which can be learned by working alongside experienced teachers in schools. The Union's insistence on the involvement of higher education in initial teacher education does not derive simply from a desire to protect the all-graduate professional status of teachers, although this is obviously crucial in the Union's view. It also arises from a clear-sighted acknowledgement that certain training functions are best located within the remit of higher education. For example, the initial selection of candidates for places on teacher training courses would, due to a lack of economies of scale, prove an onerous task for a great many schools.

Moreover, the diversification of routes into the teaching profession has been a positive development from a perspective of equality. Successful development of such routes as these has been facilitated in great part by HEIs themselves. The fact that, for example, mature entrants, returners and overseas-trained teachers can now, through a higher education course, achieve degree status on their way to becoming a qualified teacher, both enhances the status of the individual and that of the teaching profession, as moving towards being broadly representative of society as a whole.

The maintenance of a higher education location for teacher education is essential throughout all phases. The spectre of a 'Mums' army' has not entirely disappeared from view. We must, as a teacher trade union, continue to bear in mind the inequalities which exist in relation to promotion and career opportunities within the profession. The response to the establishment of pilot courses for specialist teacher assistants (STAs) has, perhaps inevitably, been characterised by the suspicion that here is a 'back-door' attempt to resurrect the original proposal for a one-year course for intending nursery and infant teachers. It will continue to be important to monitor the development of STA courses. Just as it would be disastrous to fail to protect the present graduate status of nursery and infant teachers, so it would be irresponsible to lose an important opportunity to raise the qualifications of those currently working alongside qualified teachers. What must be guarded against, however, is any suggestion that initial teacher education and enhanced training for support staff are interchangeable. Significant promotion opportunities for women teachers continue to be offered mostly in the infant sector. The removal of graduate status for those working with 3-to-7-year-olds would disadvantage large numbers of women teachers currently under-represented in management posts. Thus the assumptions, stereotyped though they are, underlying the 'Mums' army' and other similar proposals, must continue to be challenged for the threat which they pose to the quality of education received by our youngest pupils.

The dangers of allowing parochialism to characterise school-based arrangements have already been mentioned. The experience of students on school placement is, by definition, formative in nature in the sense of helping to establish a sound foundation of professional habits, which will continue to develop and to become more refined throughout a teaching career.

In 1991 HMI pointed out:

> The success of school-based training depends on the quality of the
> relationship between the training institution and the school . . . no single
> person or institution can offer all the expertise students require.
>
> (HMI, 1991)

It is always rewarding for students who, having successfully completed a
course of training, are then offered a contract by the school in which they
have been learning. What must, however, be guarded against, is the view
that school-based training is an 'on-the-job' induction into the life of just one
school.

High levels of skill and competence from teachers have never been in such
demand as they are currently. In this situation new partnership arrangements
and indeed, school-centred schemes must be about providing future members
of the teaching profession who are flexible and adaptable enough to be able
to teach a broad range of pupils in a wide variety of settings. The information
technology revolution alone is already exercising huge influences on our society
and on the way we learn. Shifts in population and, for example, closer links
with Europe and beyond, mean that the teaching workforce of the future will
be required to demonstrate levels of flexibility and responsiveness greater than
those already demanded of them. Our initial teacher education arrangements
must reflect an acknowledgement of these challenges.

There is no doubt that, as HMI stated (op.cit.), when teachers themselves
serve as models of good practice, then students benefit considerably. The
implications of new partnership arrangements are considerable, in as much
as they require of schools increasing numbers of experienced, well-informed
teachers to come forward to act as mentors. In their discussion of mentors'
contributions in initial teacher education HMI described them as involved in
the pilot arrangements for the Articled and Licensed Teacher Schemes:

> [Mentors needed] more time and better training to carry out the range
> of tasks they have undertaken . . .
>
> (ibid.)

HMI observed that:

> only rarely have mentors received training for their role and few receive
> enough, if any, extra time in which to carry it out.
>
> (ibid.)

Early evidence from new partnership arrangements suggests that these problems, identified in 1991 by HMI, still remain. What is clear is that partnerships,
as they are now evolving, will be increasingly demanding of school-based
mentors' time and expertise. There can be no guarantees of success for
partnerships if the needs of mentors for proper training and support are not
addressed.

The NUT is in no doubt that the level of resources made available to
schools must be sufficient to allow teachers to fulfil their side of partnership

arrangements, and, crucially, to protect the teaching time available for pupils. As HMI and, more recently, the Council for the Accreditation of Teacher Education (CATE) have affirmed, it must not be disregarded that the main function of a school is the education of its pupils.

It is for this reason that the NUT has always advocated that involvement in initial teacher education should be regarded as integral to a school's ongoing professional development programme and, therefore, to the school development plan itself. Teacher involvement cannot be regarded as dependent on goodwill. Where additional responsibilities are taken on by teachers they have to be recognised both by appropriate additional salary points and by appropriate allocations of time within teaching time. Widespread agreement within a school about involvement is the best guarantee of success for any scheme. However, the resources available to schools in respect of their responsibilities must be sufficient to guarantee that those responsibilities will be met in full.

Any decision about increased involvement in initial teacher education need not be based solely on consideration of the amount of money a school will receive for its responsibilities. There will be many positive examples of inventive and mutually beneficial arrangements between HEIs and schools, which can enhance financial allocations to schools. It will be important that the TTA is able, through its monitoring work, to network these examples of successful, school-based training to a wide range of schools and HEIs. Openness and fairness about costs and benefits is essential. It would not, for example, be suitable for the TTA or a teachers' organisation to be prescriptive about the amount of money schools should receive in respect of students. But what is essential is that the balance of responsibilities and the share of duties and accountability undertaken by schools must be very clearly identified from the outset.

As a trade union the NUT would not wish to advocate any position or course of action which might result in the loss of posts in HEIs. According to our own recent research findings it seems that, regrettably, this has indeed been the case in a number of institutions. (Joint NUT University of the West of England 1995.) If resources allocated in respect of initial teacher education are insufficient, then it is with a united voice that this needs to be declared. 'Short-changing' of schools by HEIs will not encourage their involvement: similarly, schools which consider turning completely away from HEIs and 'going it alone' in ITE run the risk of short-changing ITE students themselves. The signs are that, currently, every effort is being made to preserve good relationships with schools by HEIs which know that this issue of resourcing is the most crucial of all for the success of future partnerships.

It would be easy, in all this, to forget the entitlements of students who are undergoing courses of ITE. The advantages which students can bring to schools have already been discussed. The development of more school-centred schemes will have long-term implications for the quality and nature of training received by future generations of student teachers. Certainly, from the point of view of mature entrants to the profession, the attractions of increased flexibility of distance learning and school-based courses will be considerable. The challenge for the more 'traditional' courses is how to remain inviting to these important individuals, who bring with them to their initial training a great deal of experience and expertise from other fields. The challenge for schools receiving such people as students is to preserve their entitlement to a period of training, free of the inevitable pressures to which established teachers are subjected, day by day.

The NUT has advocated to the TTA that one aspect of partnership arrangments which it should be monitoring is the extent to which students on school placements retain their status of being additional to the staffing complement of the school. This is not an argument for 'arms-length' treatment by qualified teachers working alongside students, but rather one which seeks to protect the interests of both parties.

High quality initial teacher education is, after all, the foundation of high quality education, for all pupils. The development of well organised partnerships, negotiated from a base of equality between schools and HEIs, will allow all those concerned with the education and training of teachers to reflect upon the qualities required of teachers at the end of this century and the start of the twenty-first. If carried out with honesty care and mutual respect the development and growth of well-structured, partnership schemes may go some way towards providing a set of genuine answers to questions about where, how and why the best and most effective form of initial teacher education should take place.

12

SCHOOL-BASED TEACHER EDUCATION: A LOOK TO THE FUTURE

Vivienne Griffiths and Patricia Owen

What then might be the likely future for schools and HEIs in partnership? In this final chapter the main features of partnership arrangements in current and developing ITE courses will be reviewed, and some future possible directions for school-based ITE indicated. Certain problems are clearly emerging, and these will be identified, but so too are the possible benefits, particularly in the area of continuing professional development. Finally, the opportunities and threats posed by the recently established Teacher Training Agency (TTA) will be examined in the light of their stated aims and objectives.

Two major themes emerge from the previous chapters. Firstly, the emphasis on ITE as a joint enterprise, to which both schools and HEIs have distinctive and important contributions to make. Secondly, and perhaps even more striking, the provision of school-based ITE as an ideal opportunity for teachers to make significant gains in terms of continued professional training and development.

Despite many warnings to the contrary it appears that the future can be viewed with at least a little optimism: new chances are now being presented to build on and adapt existing good practices in ITE, and to consolidate and reform relationships between partners. The debate stimulated by this enterprise, in the form of the exchange of theories, interpretations, research and practice, as illustrated in the preceding pages, can only help with these positive developments.

FEATURES OF PARTNERSHIP

The greater involvement required of schools in both 'the planning and management of training courses' (DES, 1992, Annex A), and the 'shared responsibility' (ibid.) necessitated in any partnership arrangements, have given rise to a negotiation, or renegotiation, of roles and responsibilities on both sides of the partnership. This has been particularly evident at secondary level since 9/92, and is beginning to occur at primary level as well, as courses move towards meeting 14/93 requirements by September 1996.

The formalisation of partnerships through partnership agreements, and statements of student entitlement, with a clear delineation of school and HEI provision for curriculum delivery, general professional studies, assessment arrangements and other aspects of the training, are the hallmark of such negotiations taking place across the country. For many HEIs the new requirements have provided a welcome opportunity to forge closer relationships with local schools, or to engage in closer co-operation with existing school partners.

These joint undertakings, new or reformed, have usually been reinforced by the setting up of management groups or partnership steering committees, consisting of representatives from both schools and HEIs, thus emphasising the joint nature of the ITE process. For example, at Sussex University the Sussex Consortium for Teacher Education and Research was launched in February 1995, marking the new arrangements between the university and its partnership schools, and a further development in the course's thirty-year history of school-based provision.

In some ways it has been easier for courses moving into partnership for the first time to develop such partnership agreements from their initial stages through joint discussion; thereby setting up arrangements which suit both schools and HEIs, are relevant to the current situation and satisfy new regulations. For courses which have been working in a school-based way for some time it has perhaps taken more convincing of participants on both sides that changes will be beneficial, and more persuasion to move those involved into a different mode of partnership where this is needed. Traditional ways of working are often regarded as preferable because they are tried and tested, or at least taken for granted and 'comfortable' for the practitioners.

In new partnerships schools need persuading that there will be benefits to both teachers and pupils, and not just extra work on top of already heavy demands; HEI lecturers may need assurances that their role will not be undermined or abolished. Nevertheless, in all partnership arrangements, whether new or old-established, change is essential, involving in most cases a shift in the balance of power towards schools, and a rethinking of roles. As Kate Ring argues (Chapter 11), an open and explicit renegotiation of responsibilities is vital if ITE is to move forward and develop positively in the future.

As with other recent changes in schools the change process has to be managed well (McCulloch and Fidler, 1994), and managed at a pace which does not place undue pressure on those who bear the brunt of the changes at the chalk face, especially the classroom teachers and mentors. Articulating a new, shared approach to teacher education takes time to implement, particularly when improved quality of the training process and the competences of newly qualified teachers is the desired – and indeed required – result (HMI, 1991).

The models of partnership evolving nationwide vary from course to course, as previous chapters have illustrated, both in terms of the extent of partnership undertaken by participating schools, and the principle underlying the allocation of roles, ranging from the complementary approach at Oxford (McIntyre, 1990) to the more reciprocal model at UEA (Husbands, this volume). In some cases differing levels of partnership operate according to the amount of additional responsibility the schools are prepared to accept, particularly in assessing the trainee teachers. This seems to be an emerging pattern on some primary courses, for example at Newcastle (Newton, this volume), where the course is currently operating with two different levels of participation, with a corresponding difference in the transfer of resources. This is particularly true for courses in transition; it remains to be seen whether this will be deemed acceptable after 1996, or whether all courses will eventually have to move into full partnership.

PROBLEMS OF PARTNERSHIP

It has already been indicated that there has been resistance to some of the required changes in ITE in both schools and HEIs, and that much work is involved on both sides in managing these changes. Such resistance stems from fears among HEIs that their important contribution to ITE will be diminished too far or destroyed completely; in school the major concern is that their essential aim of educating children will be undermined by having to undertake too many additional training duties.

The move away from the ivory tower of the university, with educational theory unrelated to the everyday practice of the classroom, has been gradual but persistent over the last three decades and, as outlined in Chapter 1, has stemmed from academics and teachers themselves, rather than from government legislation in the first instance. Such changes came with the professionalisation of teaching and were essential to the growth of high quality teacher training; the recent Holmes report (1995) on the current state of ITE in the USA shows what can happen when a university-based system stagnates by remaining too out of touch with schools (Hodges, 1995).

Nevertheless, concerns that the government agenda is the eventual total abolition of HEI involvement in ITT give rise to passionate outcries such as the following:

> Britain is attempting to banish the training of teachers from the university. Although its government may have been given good reasons for doing so, it is certain that, if this country is to develop a teaching profession of the quality it obviously requires, such a profession needs and deserves a strong university connection.
>
> (Judge, 1995)

John Furlong (unpublished paper, 1994) points out that higher education involvement in ITE is an important means by which the essential professionalism of teaching is asserted and safeguarded. Wilkin and Sankey (1994) make a confident assertion about the importance of the university contribution:

If all university departments were destroyed then shortly new centres of expertise would arise to serve the needs of schools ... Such expertise would be based upon knowledge, experience and research – precisely the service which universities are there to give.

(Wilkin and Sankey, 1994, p. 187)

Certainly the current situation in France (Judge *et al.*, 1994) suggests that the future of HEIs in teacher training is perhaps more secure in the long term than is currently perceived: France had moved ITE away from the universities (a move much applauded by the British government), but recent changes in policy have reversed this move and brought ITE firmly back into the auspices of a rigorous academic base. Judge argues that the French example should be taken very seriously in the UK as a means of building in an assurance of a high standard of consistent quality in ITE.

Another reassuring indication of the future role for HEIs in teacher training is that schools are showing a general reluctance to relinquish their links with their higher education partners. Although patterns and degrees of partnership vary, alongside an overall move towards more school involvement, the role of the HEIs still remains strong, and the take up of the school-centred scheme (SCITT) has been slow. There is still widespread scepticism among teachers and academics that SCITT courses could fulfil all the requirements for partnership and quality in ITE, although they are to be assessed by the Office for Standards in Education (OFSTED) according to the same criteria as other courses (DFE, 1993).

However, perhaps the main reason for the lack of SCITT courses so far is the concern in schools that further involvement in ITE will detract from their main purpose in teaching children. This very real concern, together with inadequate resourcing, lack of time for mentoring, and the disruption caused to school routines generally, has led many schools across the UK to withdraw from teacher training altogether (Pyke, 1995). Lack of places in schools for incoming trainee teachers is now the most urgent problem facing ITE courses nationwide. Competition for partner schools is so severe in some parts of the country that students have to travel hundreds of miles in some cases to undertake school placements (UCET, 1995).

The funding issue, as indicated earlier in the book, is one of the strong-est and most immediate for schools considering whether or not to offer places for ITE students. At secondary level the average transfer of resources is now £1,000 per student, but schools argue that this does not meet the real costs involved. The pre-allocation of resources to ITE built into schools' forward planning also means that secondary schools now often expect payment when projected places are not taken up because of drop out. When this is coupled with widespread under-recruitment in shortage subjects such as maths, science and modern languages, HEIs are faced with a further drain on their own resources, especially if they are penal-ised for failing to meet recruitment targets. Many universities and colleges have already had to cut down on staffing as a result of these financial pressures.

At primary level payments to schools still vary enormously, from £120 to £1,000 per trainee. Some courses still make no transfer at all to primary partners; the average emerging payment seems to be £500, but there is still great fluctuation and change while courses are in transition to 14/93. Part of the discrepancy between primary and secondary payments is because the minimum number of required days in school is lower on primary courses (90 days on primary PGCE courses compared to 120 days on secondary PGCEs). There is also a requirement on primary courses that payments relate to 'the increased contribution of schools . . . over and above their existing commitment to teacher training' (DFE, 1993 p. 12), so that transfers are tied to new areas of responsibility, often still being negotiated.

Nevertheless, primary schools are now strongly asserting the need for higher payments if they are to stay in partnership, particularly in the light of the heavy new demands in providing, for example, directed time in the core curriculum subjects. As in the secondary sector, many primary schools are also withdrawing places for ITE until the funding situation is resolved. This is one area in which the recently established TTA will have a vital part to play.

THE TEACHER TRAINING AGENCY

The demise of the Council for the Accreditation of Teacher Education (CATE), and its replacement by the new government quango the Teacher Training Agency, have given rise to some trepidation among the teaching profession and training institutions. As the new funding and regulatory body, the TTA obviously has a crucial role in the future development of school-based ITE. It is understandable, therefore, that a profession which has been subject to so many recent changes should regard this new arrival on the scene with certain misgivings.

The functions and aims of the TTA are

- to fund and promote high quality teacher education;
- to accredit the providers of ITT;
- to provide information and advice about the teaching profession;
- to fund classroom-based research;
- and support continuing professional development (CPD).

With the launch of its corporate plan in March 1995 the TTA stated its intention to promote in all its activities choice, diversity, efficiency and accountability.

Perhaps because of the severity of some of the problems outlined in the previous section the TTA since its inception has been stressing the positive benefits of involvement in school-based ITE, mainly through a series of regional conferences to which representatives from schools, HEIs and local education authorities have been invited. There have also been a large number of consultation documents, the most recent of which has concerned the future funding of ITE courses on the basis of quality ratings. So far the TTA appears to be taking a pro-active, rather than simply an advisory role, and is consulting widely.

The first public address by the TTA's chief executive, Anthea Millett, given at the launch in February 1995 of the Sussex Consortium for Teacher Education and Research, exemplified this approach. At this event Anthea Millett stressed the benefits of involvement in partnership for HEIs, schools, teachers and trainee teachers. Particular points which she highlighted were enhanced skills and job satisfaction for teachers; improved understanding of teachers' professional development needs and easier access to HEIs to meet these; clearer identification of issues involved in school improvement and increased opportunities to research such issues in the classroom; and the not inconsiderable contribution which trainee teachers make to teaching placement schools.

Anthea Millett also explored ways in which school-based partnerships might be encouraged, and the quality of such partnerships secured. Strategies suggested for ensuring quality included establishing clear partnership contracts; developing performance indicators for effective partnership practice; carefully screening participants in any partnership scheme; developing classroom teachers' and mentors' skills through appropriate training; and making partnership a privilege, rather than a chore, for all involved. Enhancing the status and professionalism both of teacher training and of teachers was thus put forward as an important factor in developing more, and more successful, school-based ITE partnership schemes.

Of course, a degree of rhetoric is to be expected, particularly as part of the process of gaining acceptance, support and credibility for any new, centrally-appointed government body such as the TTA from an education community reeling from the roller coaster of so many recent, rapid and externally imposed changes. Yet seen in the context of the existing and innovative work now being carried out by those involved in all areas of school-based ITE, the picture thus presented by the chief executive of the TTA contained grounds for at least cautious optimism.

On this occasion, and at the recent conferences around the UK, the TTA has not ignored the potential problems and difficulties arising from involvement in partnership. For example, the diversity of partnership schemes between different HEIs, and the problems this could give rise to, have been recognised, especially where schools are involved in training students from a number of different HEIs, and have to accommodate a variety of training structures. Although this is not seen as an area in which it is appropriate for the TTA to intervene directly, nevertheless it is acknowledged that some guidance from the

TTA might be useful, and that co-ordination on a regional basis, already taking place in some parts of the UK, could perhaps be a useful way forward.

The TTA has also recognised the particular problems associated with funding, and is addressing them in two main ways as a priority issue. Firstly, a funding review is underway to examine current funding arrangements and the rationale behind them. In particular the survey will address the disparities in funding from one institution to another, which the chair of the TTA Geoffrey Parker described as 'indefensible' (Pyke, 1995). These largely arise because of differences in internal cross-subsidising, and lead to some ITE courses, generally in the older universities, receiving more money per student than others. The discrepancies between top-slicing arrangements across different universities also lead to considerable differences in course funding, and would be a useful area for review.

The other main way in which the TTA intends to address and alter funding arrangements is by linking the amount of money paid to the quality assessments of ITT courses. Anthea Millett stated in May 1995:

> It is time to move away from the current method of funding and allocating teacher training places which bears no relation to the quality of training ... If we are to get the high quality teachers we need we must use all our muscle to drive up the quality of the training provided.
>
> (Pyke, 1995)

The current consultation document seeks views on whether this method should be based solely on OFSTED course inspection reports, or whether courses should have an opportunity to submit self-assessments and quality bids in addition. This would be particularly relevant to secondary courses inspected one or two years ago, or recently inspected primary courses in transition, where further changes would be expected. On the other hand it might be cumbersome to administer a monitoring of bids for quality, and would give course teams yet more paperwork to submit. The TTA will reach decisions on this after the period of consultation ends in July 1995, with a view to implementing changes after the initial round of primary 'sweep' inspections by OFSTED is complete.

There are two other areas in which the TTA has a clear agenda. Firstly, the agency wishes to fund and promote classroom-based research, and is already seeking bids for the first projects on numeracy and literacy. Secondly, a nationwide survey of in-service training (INSET) has been set up, in order to gather information on:

> the perceived quality, content and relevance of training; how schools are using the five training days; the sources of funding supporting training; and the perceived effectiveness of different types of training in improving teaching and learning.
>
> (Millett 1995)

As with funding the review will also include a widespread consultation exercise, in order to identify how to 'maximise the potential of different types of training' (Millet, ibid.) for the continuing professional development (CPD) of teachers, including the benefits of ITE partnerships. The potential value of such a survey is great, if indeed clearer objectives and criteria for CPD emerge as a result. There is no doubt that the TTA intends to have a considerable impact on teacher training and the teaching profession in the immediate and longer-term future.

BENEFITS OF PARTNERSHIP

The areas being addressed by the TTA are timely given the current developments in ITE partnerships, as exemplified by common themes running through contributions to this book. In particular the potential for CPD and educational research associated with many thriving ITE partnerships affords an optimistic view.

All the previous chapters present, in different ways and within differing contexts, the benefits to practising teachers of being associated with teacher education and training, and the opportunity for enhanced professional development. For example, Jill Bourne and Jenny Leach consider classroom teachers' work with trainee teachers as 'co-operative teaching for staff development', whilst Susan Sanders identifies the particular benefits to teachers in small rural primary schools who are involved with ITE. Chris Husbands and Janice Windsor both demonstrate the positive effects and professional development potential for teachers at different levels in the partnership school. Wayne Jones makes the important suggestion that the development of forms of accreditation for mentor training might enhance and encourage teachers' involvement in mentoring as a form of professional development. Further professional qualifications for mentoring are indeed being developed in certain institutions across the UK.

The initial training period as the first stage in teachers' further professional development is also stressed in several of the chapters. For example, Jenny Harrison and Lynn Newton both stress that the acquisition of knowledge and professional skills is a continuous process throughout a teacher's career. The framework for the development of competences provided during initial training, now required by both 9/92 and 14/93, including the setting of targets for future development, can therefore be seen as a valuable starting point. Examples are being introduced in certain parts of the UK which link trainee teachers' profiles of competence to those for newly qualified teachers (East Sussex, 1994), and this can be seen as a further beneficial development from ITE partnerships.

The important contribution that teachers as well as academics can make to educational research through the training process is shown in many chapters too. For example, Paul Stephens reaffirms the principle of the reflective practitioner and the importance of school-based research; Lisa Dart and Pat Drake suggest that teachers have a central part to play in the dissemination of professional knowledge about subject pedagogy. The need for adequate mentor training and support to underpin such a vital contribution must not be overlooked, and this is particularly stressed by Kate Ring from a union perspective.

That successful partnership depends on the full involvement of both schools and HEIs working co-operatively, is well illustrated throughout *Schools in Partnership*. Hence the importance of representing both university and school-based practitioners in the book. As the contributors show the most constructive and positive way forward for ITE, whether in the primary or secondary sectors, is through the joint efforts and commitment of schools and HEIs. All the chapters reaffirm in different ways the importance of well organised, well resourced and enthusiastic partnerships to ensure high quality practice in teacher education.

With partnership schemes such as those described in the book, as well as others round the country, school-based ITE, associated research and other professional development activities have much future potential too. Despite serious worries about issues such as funding, the strength of school-based ITE is that schools and higher education institutions can operate fruitfully together in such a way as to complement, assist and inspire each other. Our hope is that such partnerships will continue to grow and develop; that their value is acknowledged and their future assured.

REFERENCES

Alexander, R. (1984) Innovation and continuity in the initial teacher education curriculum, in R. J. Alexander, M. Craft, and Lynch., (eds), *Change in Teacher Education: Context and Provision since Robbins*, Cassell, London.

Alexander, R (1990) Partnership in initial teacher education; confronting the issues, in M. Booth, V. Furlong, and M. Wilkin. (eds), *op.cit.*.

Alexander, R. and Whittaker, J. (eds.) (1980) *Developments in PGCE Courses*, Society for Research into Higher Education, Guildford.

Anzai, Y. and Simon, H. (1979) The theory of learning by doing, *Psychological Review*, 86(2), 124–140.

Aplin, R. (1994) Partnership: The Leicestershire secondary experience, in A. Williams (ed), *Perspectives on Partnership: Secondary Initial Teacher Training*, Falmer Press, London.

Ashton, P., Henderson, E. and Peacock, A. (1989) *Teacher Education through Classroom Evaluation: The Principles and Practice of IT-INSET*

Aston University and Department of the Environment (1981) The social-effects of rural primary school re-organisation in England: a study carried out on behalf of the Department of the Environment and the Department of Education and Science: Final Report. University of Aston, Birmingham.

Baker, E. (1994) In a speech by representatives from OFSTED to participants of the UCET Spring Conference, Swallow Hotel, York, 6–7 June.

Barber, M. (1993) A contribution to the joint NUT/Oxford University Conference on Initial Education, 17 March.

Barnes, L. and Shinn-Taylor, C. (1988) Teacher competency and the primary school curriculum: a survey of five schools in north-east England, *British Educational Research Journal*, Vol. 14, no. 3, pp. 283–295.

Bayliss, S. (1985) United they stand: a small school success story, *Times Educational Supplement*, 15 February, p. 8.

Beck, D. and Booth, M. (1992) The role of the mentor in Wilkin, M., *op. cit.*.

Bell, A. (1981) Structure, knowledge and social relationships in teacher education, *British Journal of Sociology of Education*, 2(1).

Bell, A. and Sigworth, A. (1987) *The Small Rural Primary School*, Falmer, Lewis.

Benton, P. (ed) (1990) *The Oxford Internship Scheme: Integration and Partnership in Initial Teacher Training*, Calouste Gulbenkian Foundation, London.

Booth, M. B., Furlong, V. J. and Wilkin, M. (eds) (1990) *Partnership in Initial Teacher Training*, Cassell, London.

Brown, G. (1985) The role of schools and teachers in teacher education, in H. Francis (ed), *Psychology in Teacher Training*, Falmer, Lewes, pp. 54–65.

Brown, S. and McIntyre, D. (1986) How do teachers think about their craft?, in M. Ben-Peretz, R. Bromme and R. Halkes (eds), *Advances in Research on Teacher Training*, ISATT and Swets and Zeitlinger BV, Lisse.

Brown, S. and McIntyre, D. (1995) *Making Sense of Teaching*, Open University Press, Buckingham.

Burgess, H. (1994) Voices on the line. Unpublished paper, Open University.

Calderhead, J. (1987) The development of knowledge structures in learning to teach, in J. Calderhead (ed), *Teachers' Professional Learning*, Falmer, Lewes, pp. 51–64.

Calderhead, J. (1992) Can the complexities of teaching be accounted for in terms of competencies? Contrasting views of professional practice from research and policy. Discussion Paper presented at UCET Annual Conference, Oxford.

Caldwell, B. J. and Spinks, J. (1989) *The Self Managing School*, Falmer, Lewes.

Carr, D. (1993) Questions of competence, *British Journal of Educational Studies*, September, Vol. XXXXI, no. 3.

Council for Accreditation of Teacher Training (1986) *Links between Initial Teacher Training Institutions and Schools, Catenote 4*, Department of Education and Science, London.

CATE (1992) *School-Based Teacher Training: Notes of Guidance for Secondary Schools and Higher Education Institutions* CATE, London.

CATE (1992) *The Accreditation of Initial Teacher Training under Circulars 9/92 (Department for Education) and 35/92 (Welsh Office) – A Note Of Guidance*, CATE, London.

Cave, J. and Cave, R. (1982) Strategies for supporting small schools, *Education 3–13*, Vol. 10, no. 1, pp. 40–43.

Chase, W. G. and Simon, H. A. (1973) Perception in chess, *Cognitive Psychology*, 4, pp. 55–81.

Clarke, K. (1992) *Speech to North of England Education Conference, Department for Education*, London, 4 January.

Clift, P. and Nuttall, D. (eds) (1987) *Studies in School Self Evaluation*, Falmer, Lewes.

Cooper, B. (1990) PGCE students and investigational approaches in secondary maths, *Research Papers in Education*, Vol. 5, no. 2 pp. 127–151.

Cox, T. and Sanders, S. (1994) *The Impact of the National Curriculum on the Teaching of Five Year Olds*, Falmer Press, London.

Crosson, M. and Shiu, C. (1994) Evaluation and judgement, in B. Jaworski and A. Watson (eds) *Mentoring in Mathematics Teaching*, for the Mathematical Association, Falmer Press, Sussex.

Dart, L. and Drake, P. (1993) School-based training: A conservative practice? *Journal of Education for Teaching*, Vol. 19, no. 2, pp. 175–189.

Dart, L. and Drake, P. (1995 forthcoming) Subject perspectives on mentoring, in H. Hagger and D. McIntyre, (eds) *Mentors in Schools: Developing the Profession of Teaching*.

Davies, I. and Macaro, E. (1995) The Reactions of Teachers, Tutors and Students to Profiling Student Competencies in Initial Teacher Education, *Journal of Further and Higher Education*. Vol. 19, no. 2.

Dean, J. (1991) *Professional Development in School*, Open University, Buckingham.

Dearing, R. (1993). *The National Curriculum and its Assessment: An Interim Report*, NCC/SEAC, London.

Department of Education and Science (1967) *Primary Education in Wales: A report of the Central Advisory Council for Education (Wales) (Gittins Report)*, HMSO, London.

Department of Education and Science (1967a) *Children and Their Primary Schools (Plowden Report)*, HMSO, London.

Department of Education and Science (1984) *Statistics of Education: Teachers in Service, England and Wales*, HMSO, London.

Department of Education and Science (1972) *Teacher Education and Training (James Report)*, HMSO, London.
Department of Education and Science (1983) *Teaching Quality*, HMSO, London.
Department of Education and Science (1984) *Initial Teacher Training: Approval of Courses*, Circular 3/84 April, HMSO, London.
Department of Education and Science (1988) *Qualified Teacher Status: A Consultation Document*, HMSO, London.
Department of Education and Science (1989a) *Articled Teacher Pilot Scheme: Invitation to Bid for Funding*, HMSO, London.
Department of Education and Science (1989b), *Initial Teacher Training: Approval of Courses*, Circular 24/89, HMSO, London.
Department of Education and Science (1989) *Discipline in Schools (The Elton Report)* London: HMSO.
Department of Education and Science (1989) *Initial Teacher Training: Approval of Courses*, Circular 24/89, HMSO, London.
Department for Education (1992) *Initial Teacher Training: Secondary Phase* Circular 9/92, HMSO, London.
Department for Education (1993) *The Initial Training of Primary School Teachers: New Criteria for Courses*, Circular 14/93, HMSO, London.
Department for Education (1993) *The Government's Proposals for the Reform of Initial Teacher Training*, HMSO, London.
Department for Education (1993b) *School-Centred Initial Teacher Training Scheme (SCITT)*, HMSO, London.
Department for Education (1994) *Personal Communication*, HMSO, London.
Department for Education (1994) *Remit Letter for the Teacher Training Agency*, HMSO, London.
Drake, P. and Dart, L. (1994) English, mathematics and mentors, in I. Reid *et al.* (eds) *Teacher Education Reform: Current Research*, Paul Chapman, London.
East Sussex C. C. (1994) *Profile for Newly Qualified Teachers*, E. Sussex.
Eggleston, J. (1985) Subject centred and school based teacher training in the PGCE, in D. Hopkins and K. Reid (eds.) *Rethinking Teacher Education*, Croom Helm, Beckenham.
Elliott, J. (1976) Preparing teachers for classroom accountability, *Education for Teaching*, 100, pp. 49–71.
Elliott, J. (1985) Facilitating action research in schools: some dilemmas, in R. G. Burgess (ed), *Feld Methods in the Study of Education*, Falmer, London.
Elliott, J. (1990) *Action Research for Educational Change*, Open University Press, Milton Keynes.
Elliott, J. (1991) Coherence and continuity in teacher education, unpublished paper, Universities Council for the Education of Teachers' conference.
Eraut, M. (1994) *Developing Professional Knowledge and Competence*, Falmer Press, Sussex.
Eraut, M. (1994) Concepts of Competence and the Deparment of Employment Contribution, paper for British Education Research Association (BERA) conference, September.
Evans, A. (1994) Taking Responsibility for the Training Curriculum within the School: The View of a Professional Tutor, in M. Wilkin and D. Sankey, *Collaboration and Transition in Initial Teacher Training*, Kogan Page, London.
Everton, T. and Impey, G. (eds) (1989) *IT-INSET: Partnership in Training, The Leicestershire Experience*, David Fulton, London.
Field, B. (1993) The past role of the teacher: Supervision as socialisation, in B. and T. Field (eds), *Teachers as Mentors*, Falmer, Lewes, pp. 46–62.

Field, B. and Field, T. (1994): *Teachers as Mentors: A Practical Guide* Falmer Press, London.

Fish, D. (1989) *Learning through Practice in Initial Teacher Training*, Kogan Page, London.

Fitzgerald, A. (1984) Two's company, *Times Educational Supplement*, 9 March, p. 26.

Fuller, F. (1970) *Personalized Education for Teachers: One Application of the Teacher Concern Model*, University of Texas R & D Centre for Teacher Education, Austin, Texas.

Furlong, V. J., Hirst, P. H., Pocklington, K. and Miles, S. (1988) *Initial Teacher Training and the Role of the School*, Open University Press, Milton Keynes.

Furlong, V. J., Wilkin, M. and Booth, M. B. (eds) (1990) *Partnership in Initial Teacher Education*, Cassell, London.

Furlong, J. and Maynard, T. (1995) *Mentoring Student Teachers: The Growth of Professional Knowledge*, Routledge, London.

Furlong, V. J. and Maynard, T. (1993) Learning to teach and models of mentoring, in D. McIntyre, H. Hagger and M. Wilkin, (eds), *Mentoring in Schools*, Kogan Page, London.

Furlong, J. (1995) Higher education and initial teacher training: a changing relation, in D. Kerr and C. O'Neill (eds) *Professional Preparation and Professional Development in a Climate of Change*: SCHTE, in association with University College of St Martin, Lancaster and University of Wales, Swansea.

Furlong, J. (1994) The rise and the rise of the mentor in British initial teacher training, in R. Yeomans and J. Sampson (eds), *Mentorship in the Primary School*, Falmer Press, London

Galton, M. and Patrick, H. (eds) (1990) *Curriculum Provision in the Small Primary School*, Routledge, London.

Garnham, A. and Oakhill, J. (1994) *Thinking and Reasoning* Blackwell, Oxford.

Goodyear, R. Little, V. (1993) *The Principles and Key Issues which Should Inform Arrangements for the Initial Education and Training of Teachers Working in Primary Schools*, General Teaching Council.

Government Statistical Services (1994) *Education Statistics for the United Kingdom*; 1993 Edition HMSO, London.

Hagger, H. and McIntyre, D. (1993). Teachers' expertise and models of mentoring, in D. McIntyre, H. Hagger and M. Wilkin, (eds), *Mentoring in Schools* Kogan Page, London.

Halliwell, S. (1988) The role of the PGCE method tutor, *Cambridge Journal of Education*, 18, 3.

Handal, G. and Lauvas, P. (1993). The practical theory of teaching, in E. Whitelegg, J. Thomas and S. Tresman (eds), *Challenges and Opportunities for Science Education*, Paul Chapman, London, pp. 79–106.

Hargreaves, A. (1992) Cultures of Teaching: a Focus for change, in A. Hargreaves, M.G. Fullan, (eds), *Understanding Teacher Development*, Cassell, London, pp. 216–40.

Hargreaves, D. (1990) *The Future of Teacher Education*, Hockerill Lecture, Hockerill Educational Foundation, Essex.

Hargreaves, D. and Hopkins, D. (1991) *The Developing School: Guidelines for School Development Planning*, Cassell, London.

Hargreaves, A. (1995) Towards a social geography of teacher education, in N. K. Shimahara and I. Z. Holowinsky. *Teacher Education in Industrialised Nations: Issues in Changing Social Contents*, Garland, New York.

Hirst, P. H. (1979) Professional studies in initial teacher education: some conceptual issues, in R. Alexander and E. Wormald (eds), *Professional Studies in Teaching*, Society for Research in Higher Education.

HMI (1991) *School-based Initial Teacher Training in England and Wales: A Report by HM Inspectorate*, HMSO, London.

HMI (1994) *University of Newcastle upon Tyne School of Education Secondary PGCE and Primary PGCE Inspection May and October 1993*, Draft report, April.

Hodges, L. (1995) Training colleges told to buck up, *The Times Educational Supplement*, 10 February.

Holmes Group (1995) *Tomorrow's Schools of Education*, Michigan State University.

Howells, R. A. (1982) *Curriculum Provision in the Small Primary School*, Cambridge Institute of Education.

Judge, H. (1994) Stop this roller-coaster ride for training, *The Times Educational Supplement*, December, p. 15.

Judge, H. (1994) Marching to Napoleon's tune, *The Times Higher Education Supplement*, 16 December.

Judge, H., Le Mosse, M., Paine, L. and Sedlake, M. (1994) *The University and the Teachers: France, the United States, England*, Oxford Studies in Comparative Education, Vol. 4 (1/2), Triangle Books.

Keast, D. (1991) *Small Schools after ERA: 1991 Survey*, University of Exeter School of Education.

Kelly, M., Beck T. and ap Thomas, J. (1992) Mentoring as a staff development activity, in Wilkin, M., *op. cit.*.

Lacey, C. (1977) *The Socialization of Teachers*, Methuen, London.

Lacey, C. and Lamont, W. (1975) *Partnership with Schools: An Experiment in Teacher Education*, Occasional Paper 5, University of Sussex Education Area.

Larkin, J. H. (1979) Information processing models and science instruction, in J. Lockhead and J. Clement (eds), *Cognitive Process Instruction*, Franklin Institute Press, Philadelphia, pp. 109–118.

Larkin, J. H. (1983) The role of problem representation in physics, in D. Gentner and A. L. Stevens (eds), *Mental Models*, Lawrence Erlbaum Associates, Hillsdale, NJ, pp. 75–98.

Lawlor, S. (1990) *Teachers Mistaught*, Centre for Policy Studies, London.

Lewis, C. G. (1991) Teaching Headships: A case study of three small primary schools Unpublished M. Ed, Dissertation, University of Wales, Swansea.

Mackinnon, A. M. (1993) Detecting reflection-in-action among preservice elementary science teachers, in E. Whitelegg, J. Thomas and S. Tresman (eds), *Challenges and Opportunities for Science Education*, Paul Chapman, London, pp. 44–60.

Maclure, S. (1993) Platform, *The Times Educational Supplement*, 18 June.

Maynard, T. and Furlong, J. (1992) Learning to Teach and Models of Mentoring, in D. McIntyre, H. Hagger, and M. Wilkin, (eds), *Mentoring: Perspectives on School-Based Teacher Education*, Kogan Page, London.

McCullough, M. and Fidler, B. (1994) *Improving Initial Teacher Education*, Longman, Essex.

McIntyre, D. (1980) The contribution of research to quality in teacher education, in E. Hoyle, and J. Megarry, (eds), *World Yearbook of Education 1980*, Professional Development of Teachers.

McIntyre, D. (1990) The Oxford internship in terms of the Cambridge analytical framework, in V. J. Furlong, M. Wilkin and M. B. Booth, *Partnership in Initial Teacher Education*, London, Cassell.

McIntyre, D. (1987) Designing a teacher education curriculum from research and theory on teacher knowledge, in J. Calderhead, (ed), *Teachers' Professional Learning*; Falmer, Lewes, pp. 97–114.

McIntyre, D. (1994) Classrooms as learning environments for student teacher, in M. Wilkin and D. Sankey (eds), *Collaboration and Transition in Initial Teacher Training*, Kogan Page, London, pp. 81–97.

McIntyre, D. (1990) Ideas and principles guiding the internship scheme, in P. Benton (ed), *The Oxford Internship Scheme*, Gulbenkian Foundation, London.

McIntyre, D., Hagger, H. and Wilkin, M. (eds) (1993) *Mentoring: Perspectives on School-Based Teacher Education*, Kogan Page, London.

McIntyre, D., Hagger, H. and Burn, K. (1994) *The Management of Student Teachers' Learning: A Guide for Professional Tutors in Secondary Schools*, Kogan Page, London.

McNair, A. (1944) *Teachers and Youth Leaders (the Mcnair Report)*, HMSO, London.

Menter, I. (1989) Teaching practice stasis: racism, sexism and school experience in initial teacher education, *British Journal of Sociology of Education*, Vol. 10, no. 4.

Millet, A. (1995) Have your say on future of training, *The Times Educational Supplement*, 19 May, p. 18.

Newton, L. D. (1994) The new primary teacher: reflections on PGCE training in I. Reid, H. Constable, and R. Griffiths (eds), *Teacher Education Reform: The Research Evidence*, Paul Chapman, London, pp. 188–196.

Nias, J. (1976) School-supervised practice in junior schools, *Trends in Education*, March (1), pp. 23–27.

NUT (1994) *Initial Teacher Education – Advice to Members on Partnership Schemes and SCITTS*.

OFSTED (1993) *The New Teacher in School*.

O'Hara, M. (1994) 'Training and the schools: responses and ripostes, *Primary Teaching Studies*, 8(1), pp. 20–24.

Patrick, H., Bernbaum, G. and Reid, K. (1982) *The Structure and Process of Initial Teacher Education within Universities in England and Wales (the SPITE Report)*, University of Leicester School of Education.

Patrick, H. (1991) Teachers in small primary schools, *Aspects of Education*, Vol. 44, pp. 58–71.

Pendry, A. (1990) The process of change in Benson, P. (ed), *The Oxford Internship Scheme: Integration and Partnership in Initial Teacher Education*, Calouste Gulbenkian Foundation, London.

Potter, A. and William, M. (1994) Clustering in small primary schools: an organisational case study, *School Organisation*, Vol. 14, no. 2, pp. 141–152.

Priest, A. G. and Lindsay, R. H. (1992) New light on novice-expert differences in physics problem solving, *British Journal of Psychology*, 83, pp. 389–405.

Pyke, N. (1995) Staffing shortage 'caused by' reforms, *The Times Educational Supplement*, 20 January, front page.

Ruthven, K. (1993) Pedagogical knowledge and the training of mathematics teachers, *Mathematics Review*, Vol. 3.

Sanders, S. E. (1994) Mathematics and mentoring, in B. Jaworski and A. Watson (eds) *Mentoring in Mathematics Teaching*, Falmer Press, London.

Sarason, S. (1993) *The Case for Change: Rethinking the Preparation of Educators*, Jossey-Bass, San Francisco.

Sayer, J. (1989) *Managing Schools*, Hodder and Stoughton, London.

Schon, D. (1983) *The Reflective Practitioner: How Professionals Think in Action*, Basic Books, New York.

Shaw, R. (1992) *Teacher Training in Secondary Schools*, Kogan Page, London.

Simon, B. (1980) Education: the new perspective, in P. Gordon (ed), *The Study of Education, Volume 2*, Woburn Press, London.

Smith, P. and West-Burnham, J. (eds) (1993) *Mentoring in the Effective School*, Longman, Essex.

Standing Conference of Principals (SCOP): Education Bill Primary ITT Questionnaire: Commentary on Findings (SCOP, Cheltenhan 1994).

Stenhouse, L. (1975) *An Introduction to Curriculum Research and Development*, Heinemann, London.
Sutton (1975) Theory in the classroom, *British Journal of Teacher Education*, 1(3).
Thiessen, D. (1992) Classroom-based teacher development in A. Hargreaves and M. G. Fullan, *Understanding Teacher Development*, Cassell, London.
Tickle, L. (1987) *Learning Teaching, Teaching Teaching: A Study of Partnership in Teacher Education*. Falmer, Lewes.
Tomlinson, J. (1995) Universities challenged, review, *The Times Educational Supplement*, 20 January, p. 16.
Tysome, T. (1994) Teacher scheme 'failing', *Times Higher Education Supplement*, no. 1130, 7 July, multimedia section p. i.
UCET (1994) *Developing Partnerships in Initial Teacher Education*, circular to HEIs and school partners.
UCET (1995) Survey reported in *The Times Educational Supplement*, 20 January.
The University of the West of England, Bristol and the NUT (1995) 'Reform' in Initial Teacher Training: the views of teachers and the implementation of partnership. Interim Report, April.
Watkins, C. and Whalley, C. (1993) Mentoring beginner teachers – issues for schools to anticipate and manage, *School Organisation*, Vol. 13, no. 2, pp. 129–138.
Welsh Office (1993) *The Initial Training of Primary School Teachers: New Criteria for Courses (Circular 62/93)*, WO, Cardiff.
West Glamorgan County Council (1985) *Resourcing the Small School: A Report by the Primary Curriculum Working Group*. West Glamorgan County Council, Swansea.
Wilkin, M. (1987) The sociology of education and the theory-practice relationship in teacher training, in P. Woods and A. Pollard (eds), *Sociology and the Teacher*, Croom Helm, London.
Wilkin, M. (1990) The development of partnership in the United Kingdom, in M. Booth, J. Furlong and M. Wilkin (eds), *Partnership in Initial Teacher Training*, Cassell, London.
Wilkin, M. (1993) School-based teacher education as a post-modern development, in D. McIntyre, H. Hagger and M. Wilkin (eds), *Mentoring*, Kogan Page, London.
Wilkin, M. and Sankey, D. (1994) *Collaboration and Transition in Initial Teacher Training*, Kogan Page, London.
Wiliam, D. (1994) I'm sorry but there's not enough money for a third teaching practice visit, in Reid *et al.* op. cit.
Willis, P. (1977) *Learning to Labour: How Working Class Kids Get Working Class Jobs*, Saxon House, Farnborough.
Wilson, P. S. and Pring, R. (1975) Editorial introduction, *London Educational Review*, 4(2/3).
Wragg, E. (1990) The Two Routes into Teaching in M. Booth, J. Furlong and M. Wilkin (eds) *Partnership in Initial Teacher Training*, Cassell, London pp. 24–32.
Wragg, E. C. (1993) *Primary Teaching Skills*, Routledge, London.
Wragg, E., Bennett, S. N. and Carre, C. (1989) Primary teachers and the National Curriculum, *Research Papers in Education*, Vol. 4, no. 3, pp. 17–45.
Yekovich, F. R., Thompson, M. A. and Walker, C. H. (1991) Generation and verification of inferences by experts and trained nonexperts, *American Educational Research Journal*, 28(1), 189–209.
Yeomans, R. and Sampson, J. (eds) (1994) *Mentorship in the Primary School*, Falmer Press, London.

INDEX